WORLD CLASS
MARRIAGE

WORLD CLASS MARRIAGE

How to Create the Relationship You Always Wanted with the Partner You Already Have

Patty Howell
and
Ralph Jones

Rowman & Littlefield Publishers, Inc.
Lanham • Boulder • New York • Toronto • Plymouth, UK

Published by Rowman & Littlefield Publishers, Inc.
A wholly owned subsidary of The Rowman & Littlefield Publishing Group, Inc.
4501 Forbes Boulevard, Suite 200, Lanham, Maryland 20706
http://www.rowmanlittlefield.com

Estover Road, Plymouth PL6 7PY, United Kingdom

British Library Cataloguing in Publication Information Available

Library of Congress Cataloging-in-Publication Data

Howell, Patty, 1943-
  World class marriage : how to create the relationship you always wanted
with the partner you already have / Patty Howell and Ralph Jones.
     p. cm.
  Includes bibliographical references and index.
  ISBN 978-1-4422-0325-9 (cloth : alk. paper) — ISBN 978-1-4422-0327-3
(electronic)
  1. Married people—Psychology. 2. Marriage—Psychological aspects. I.
Jones, Ralph, 1923- II. Title.
  HQ734.H895 2010
  306.872—dc22

                                                        2009047319

∞™ The paper used in this publication meets the minimum requirements of
American National Standard for Information Sciences—Permanence of Paper
for Printed Library Materials, ANSI/NISO Z39.48-1992.

Printed in the United States of America

CONTENTS

ACKNOWLEDGMENTS

Perhaps the greatest advantage in writing this book has been the opportunity to teach communication skills to thousands of people in countries around the world. From this extensive experience on four continents, we have gained innumerable insights about our fellow human beings as they struggle to make their relationships work. The greatest of these is the sure knowledge that we are more similar in our needs than we are separated by our differences. We have been warmed by people's hearts and educated by their willingness to share with us. This book benefits from the richness of those experiences. We thank Dr. Thomas Gordon and his Effectiveness Training programs and the California Healthy Marriages Coalition (CHMC) for these unparalleled opportunities to teach and learn.

We have also educated ourselves with many personal growth experiences that have contributed greatly to this book. These experiences—classes, workshops, seminars, groups, therapy—have also propelled our growth as individuals and nurtured our relationship in countless important ways. "The best investment you can make is in yourself" is a saying that rings profoundly true in our lives, and we strongly endorse personal growth as a foundational investment for being able to create a world class marriage.

We are grateful to CHMC President Dennis Stoica for early championing of our World Class Marriage Workshop for couples and for fostering widespread adoption of this program throughout California, as well as to CHMC partnering organizations headed by Ariel Meza, Bishop John Sanchez, Dr. Eun Soon Yang, David D'Leon, and Daniel and Liz Ballon, who were early and enthusiastic supporters of the World Class Marriage program.

We are most grateful to Jeanne Fredericks, our literary agent, who has distinguished and endeared herself to us in many ways, including her conscientious shopping and shepherding of our manuscript and her unfailingly classy and trustworthy professionalism. We feel most fortunate to have Jeanne as our agent. We are delighted to have Rowman & Littlefield publish our work and thank our editor, Suzanne Staszak-Silva, for recognizing its unique value amid a crowded field of marriage and relationship books and for supporting its publication.

Finally, we want to thank Diane Sollee, founder and director of the Coalition for Marriage, Family, and Couples Education, as well as the Smart Marriages Conference and listserv, who recognized the importance of working in preventive ways to help couples learn how to create healthy and satisfying relationships, coined the term "marriage education," and began and fostered the formation of what is now an international infrastructure of marriage support programs and providers. She should be regarded as a heroine for marriages and families and a national treasure.

DEFINITION OF A
WORLD CLASS MARRIAGE

A world class marriage is a dynamic and special relationship filled with love, caring, and trust, grounded in the knowledge that both partners bring to that relationship a commitment to ways of living and loving that nurture the growth, happiness, and satisfaction for both.

PREFACE

No goal is as universally shared as the desire to have a happy marriage—a satisfying, intimate relationship with a cherished loved one. We have encapsulated people's goals for great satisfaction with this relationship as having a world class marriage.

As a first requirement for such an achievement, both partners must value the relationship, wish to keep it, and wish to make it as satisfying as possible. Still, despite the great desire that most couples have to succeed together, the U.S. divorce rate remains close to 50 percent, and divorces are increasing throughout the world. Moreover, divorced people who marry a second time run an even greater risk of divorcing their second spouse. It's clear that true love, the best of intentions, and doing what comes naturally provide couples with much less than what is required for long-term happiness together.

The carnage that results from widespread marital failure cascades into what we now believe is a serious social epidemic. In addition to the considerable psychological pain of divorce, there are additional negative consequences to the couple's financial stability, job productivity, and mental and physical health. Furthermore, we now know that children of divorced parents are at increased risk for academic problems, emotional and physical issues, and problems with their social relationships. What are experienced privately as personal or family problems cumulatively become problems of tremendous significance to our society and our economy. The latest estimate of the cost of family fragmentation to taxpayers across America is $112 billion a year, an estimate considered conservative.[1] This is no small matter.

Our intent with this book is to empower couples with practical knowledge and skills, which are seldom learned at our parents' knees or from the popular culture, in order to create deeply satisfying and enduring relationships.

Thanks to groundbreaking relationship research that has been conducted over the past several decades, we now know, more than any previous generation, what it takes to make a relationship flourish. Yet this important knowledge is largely buried in professional literature of which most couples are unaware.

The insights in *World Class Marriage* are distilled from this literature, from our experience teaching relationship skills around the world, and from our own successful marriage of more than thirty years. Whether you are still in the honeymoon phase or in a mature relationship, we now share with you the most powerful and practical ways to help you move toward a world class marriage.

INTRODUCTION

THE NATURE OF MARRIAGE

Love may be blind, but marriage is a real eye-opener.

—Anonymous

Finding a partner, someone with whom you can share your life, is one of life's grand pursuits. Our adolescence and early adulthood are spent learning how to identify, attract, and "catch" the right person. Finding someone who is attractive to us and who finds us attractive is an experience of great intensity, filled with excitement and profound feelings of validation as a human being. This saturation in happiness is its own reward. You and this wonderful other person share interests in common, you like each other, love each other, want to spend your lives together—what else could you ask for?

Very few of us ask for much more than this. Yet life presents us with opportunities and challenges of profound complexity, and the marriage relationship is the one through which we most deeply experience the whole range of life's joys and sorrows. Therefore, the marriage relationship has a profound bearing on who we are, how we relate to the world, what our options are, what roads we travel—the very essence and substance of our life.

In American culture, finding a partner and falling in love is about romance, attraction, hormones, excitement, fantasy, dreams, illusion, and hope. Once we have found our partner and made a commitment to the relationship, we settle down comfortably as a duo. Then from out of somewhere, life comes along. Our jobs ask more of us, children bring multiple challenges, we may have to deal with health and financial issues, or any number of complex challenges, both from within and from outside of the relationship. Some of these challenges are of enormous consequence. Thus the marriage relationship, which was founded upon excitement and attraction, happiness and hope, optimism and ease, now is being asked to provide the emotional foundation for each partner's capacity to create—from decades of challenge and chance—a life of success and satisfaction.

Do the hormone-charged relationship decisions of our early adulthood set us up for marital disappointment? Not necessarily, but from the perspective of five, ten, or twenty years down the marriage road, most people will agree that they entered into marriage with a heavy dose of naïveté.

The Honeymoon

In any relationship, the honeymoon lasts approximately six to eighteen months. If you're lucky, it might even last for two years. This honeymoon has nothing to do with marriage; it refers to the excitement and joys of any new relationship. This affects how easy or difficult it is to overlook certain behaviors of the other person. You know the honeymoon is over when you realize that your partner is not perfect, that she or he has some annoying characteristics that you don't like. This is when you realize that your beloved can aggravate you in some respects, despite many other wonderful characteristics. This is when the real work of relationship building begins.

Sadly, many people don't know how to build a successful relationship with a flawed human being. And the truth is, everyone who wishes to be in a relationship has to build one with a flawed human being.

World Class Marriage builds on the premise that all human beings are flawed and that all relationships have conflict. It is how well people express their needs, hear their partner's needs, resolve conflicts, and face life's complex challenges together that determine how satisfying the relationship is. If you don't handle these situations skillfully and in ways that enhance the experience of being together, the predictable outcome is frustration and resentment, which can ultimately mean the end of the relationship. When each partner is able to get his or her needs met in the relationship, grow as a human being, and know that conflicts and disagreements will be resolved to the satisfaction of each, the relationship deepens profoundly. It is through this process that we come to experience satisfaction, closeness, relationship growth, and a deep and true love for our partner—a world class marriage.

Marriage as Who You Are

We, Patty and Ralph, have taught relationship skills to thousands of people in workshops around the world, helping them improve relationships with their children, colleagues, friends, and each other. Yet it was not until we started working with couples that we recognized clearly the primacy of the marriage relationship in defining for people who they are and whether their life is satisfying. People with problems at work or problems with their children certainly experience concern, anxiety, pain, and other difficult feelings. Yet these relationships, however important, still remain some distance from our inner core. Nothing defines who we are and how happy we are with the same intensity and vividness as our primary relationship—our marriage, whether formalized or not.

Even the relationship with our parents eventually takes a backseat to our marriage in defining who we are. Our child-parent relationship looms very large during the first twenty years or so. After that, when we are on our own, our development as a person continues, and we come to view our childhood as "then" and not "who I am now." Although we model after our parents strongly and inherit many tendencies from them, we generally define ourselves as being different from our parents. The impact of the marriage relationship on our identity is so strong that after many years, the sense of merged identity, of sharing a fate together despite dramatically different personality characteristics causes many people to feel at one with their partner. The sense of "we-ness" can be profound, regardless of whether or not you are happy together.

For those who become unhappy in their relationship, this sense of blended identity can feel like a trap. It can seem like fate dealt a cruel blow in bringing you together. After the honeymoon, that dreamboat husband or fairy princess wife turns out to be just a regular person with some assets and liabilities, some attractive qualities that fit easily with your own personality, and some problematic ones that clash badly. Sometimes our partner's problematic qualities seem likely to doom the relationship, and sometimes it's our own problems.

Relationships and Growth

Fate hasn't played you a trick. Those powerful hormones serve somehow to smooth the path, helping us overcome the fears that most of us have about entering into a serious, committed relationship. If the attraction is strong enough (and whatever rational thoughts we have also okay the deal), the hormones help us make a scary, important life decision—to become part of a couple.

So we get married or somehow create a committed relationship with our new partner and experience the joys of the honeymoon phase. When the blinding intensity of that honeymoon cools down, we have the opportunity to begin building a permanent and even more rewarding life together. The opportunities we have will try us, test us, frustrate us, grow us, and define us in the most profound ways. The relationship becomes a perpetual game board upon which we face the challenges of life, in which growth—both for the individual and the relationship—is the desired outcome.

This, the greatest of games, challenges you in ways you cannot imagine when you start the relationship. Over time, you will share successes and failures, health and sickness, and gains and losses of sometimes overwhelming proportions. For those who want to develop greater proficiency in playing the game and to derive greater satisfaction from the process, *World Class Marriage* is designed to be a reliable operator's manual.

What most of us want in our post-honeymoon relationship is a partner who can be there—reliably—for us as we go through life. And the truth is, no one is a great partner at the start of the relationship. All of us have many things to learn. Life is about learning, and marriage is about learning together how to face complex challenges successfully and doing so in ways that enhance you both as individuals and your relationship as a couple.

Let's be grateful for the hormones that give us the courage to start a life together and that continue to bring great pleasure and happiness. Let's also recognize the critical nature of a marriage relationship with its profound impact on all aspects of our life. Let's acknowledge that learning to have a world class marriage is the challenge of our lifetime. And let's give thanks to that brave person who's agreed to partner with us as we learn how to create a dynamic and satisfying life together.

THE STRUCTURE OF A WORLD CLASS MARRIAGE

What Works and What Doesn't

> Life is rich, always changing, always challenging, and . . . architects have the task . . . of transforming human aspirations into habitable and meaningful space.
>
> —Arthur Erickson

Most people don't really know what it takes to make a marriage work, although magazines, popular books, and talk shows overflow with advice. This advice is sometimes contradictory and often based solely on well-intentioned personal biases or points of view. Lacking clarity about this important facet of their personal lives, most couples try conscientiously to succeed in their relationship together but don't have the confidence that they know what it takes to ride the bull successfully. They end up holding on tight and hoping for the best.

Diane Sollee, founder and director of the Coalition for Marriage, Family, and Couples Education, says that a crucial factor in helping people get past the sense that success in marriage is based on chance is to recognize that marriage is a skill-based relationship.[2] Yet for most of human civilization, there has been very little solid data about factors that affect marital outcomes and the skills necessary to preserve marriages.

For more than thirty years John Gottman and his colleagues at the University of Washington have engaged in pioneering work, studying hundreds of couples interacting together in an apartment-like setting they call the "Love Lab." Their data yield clarity about the behaviors that are associated with marital failure.[3] These data are so valuable to our species that we believe they should be better known.

Astonishingly, Gottman and his colleagues have identified seven behaviors that allow them to predict future divorce with more than 90 percent accuracy after observing a couple discuss an issue in their marriage for just five minutes. These seven predictors of divorce are:

1. A "harsh start" in an argument—immediately becoming negative and accusatory when confronting your partner;
2. Criticism—saying negative things about your partner's character or personality;
3. Contempt—sneering, sarcasm, cynicism, name-calling, mockery, hostile humor, disgust;
4. Defensiveness—justifying your behavior, attacking your partner instead;
5. Stonewalling—disengaging, turning away, refusing or becoming unable to speak or react;
6. Flooding—a physiological response to your partner's negativity, characterized by increased heart rate, secretion of adrenaline, increased blood pressure, and a sense of being overwhelmed;
7. Failed repair attempts—attempts by one partner to repair damage and keep negativity from escalating, which are ignored or otherwise met with failure.

Gottman's data also identify six predictors of success:

1. High levels of friendship, respect, affection, and humor—ingredients we all readily understand as important;
2. A ratio of 20:1 or better positive interactions compared with negative interactions during your everyday life together; and maintaining a ratio of 5:1 or better during times of conflict;

3. Successful "bids for attention"—when your partner tries to get your attention, he or she is generally successful;
4. Soft starts to disagreements—initiating confrontations in ways that don't cause immediate damage;
5. A husband who accepts influence from his wife—although women are traditionally trained to accept influence from their husbands, we've never met a wife who didn't also want to be able to influence her husband;
6. Partners who are aware of and respect each other's needs, likes, dislikes, and their inner life.

Gottman's data tell us what does and doesn't work—the common behaviors that help a marriage flourish and those that can bring a marriage down like a house of cards. If you wish to create a world class marriage, Gottman's data give you a clear fix on what to do and what to avoid at all costs.

Are there other ingredients that help a marriage grow? A marriage is a complex organism, a living structure. Strong structures need firm foundations. It is not enough to avoid the behaviors that predict the destruction of marriage. We believe it is essential to incorporate into your relationship three guiding attitudes or fundamental postures toward your spouse that have been proven to support his or her growth as a fully functioning human being—empathy, acceptance, and genuineness.

Carl Rogers's pioneering person-centered approach to psychotherapy, developed in the 1940s, spawned a fascinating series of research studies with profound implications for couples.[4] These studies showed that, independent of the theoretical orientation of a therapist, the most important factors predicting the capacity of a client to deal successfully with his or her problems were the extent to which the therapist provided empathy, acceptance, and genuineness. Related studies conducted over the past several decades yielded results that are so convincing that these three conditions are now accepted by professionals as both necessary and sufficient for personal growth. From our professional work and personal experiences in our own relationship, we are convinced of the importance of these conditions as the bedrock of what is required for a world class marriage.

THE STRUCTURE OF A WORLD CLASS MARRIAGE

WORLD CLASS MARRIAGE

Setting Goals	Avoiding Blame	Understanding the Nature of Behavior	Using Power Listening	Giving Up Tit for Tat	Assuming Self-Responsibility	Avoiding Cool Talk	Changing Behaviors, Not Your Partner	Knowing When to Surrender	Giving Caring the Way It Matters	Handling Hot Topics	Resolving Conflicts & Disagreements	Giving Apology & Forgiveness	Growing Yourself	Forging a Bond	Nurturing the Honeymoon
1	2	3	4	5	6	7	8	9	10	11	12	13	14	15	16

EMPATHY - ACCEPTANCE - GENUINENESS

Showing The 16 Pillars,
Undergirded by the Three Conditions for Growth,
Supporting a World Class Marriage

Figure I

Upon the foundation of empathy, acceptance and genuineness, we have identified sixteen key pillars that are necessary to support and elevate a relationship to what we consider world class status. Undergirded by the three conditions that support growth, the 16 Pillars create an operating system that nurtures the growth of the relationship and the people who share it (see figure 1). These pillars and conditions equip us to become architects of our own relationship, "transforming human aspirations into habitable and meaningful space."

I

THE 16 PILLARS OF A
WORLD CLASS MARRIAGE

We will now explore the 16 Pillars and learn how to operationalize them, and we invite you to join us in creating that meaningful space for your own world class marriage.

I

PILLAR I

SETTING GOALS

He turns not back who is bound to a star.

—Leonardo da Vinci

A famous *New Yorker* magazine cartoon shows a man happily lying stretched out on a couch, shoes off, eyes shut, half asleep, when his wife suddenly sweeps into the room, clipboard in hand, proclaiming, "If it's all right with you, I thought we'd do some long-range planning tonight."

The idea of long-range planning and setting big goals may be about as welcome to some couples as it obviously was to the guy in the cartoon—that is to say, not at all. But well-defined goals can be a key ingredient to the success of a marriage. Sociology professor Pepper Schwartz's study of six thousand couples confirmed that very successful couples have something more together—in addition to their children—that brings enjoyment to their relationship.[5]

Without goals, couples tend to drift, time passes by without real meaning, and the relationship is not nurtured by the joys of hard-won accomplishments and shared delights. With them, partners' lives are rescued from sameness and boredom, from petty complaints and bickering, as they strive to reach their own personal star.

Of course, a marriage comes equipped with a few built-in goals. These usually include building a happy life together, making enough money to support yourselves, advancing your careers, and, in most marriages, having and raising successful children. Those are the basics.

Beyond those lie the dreams and desires that make your lives and your relationship unique, that stretch you, that involve you in something bigger than everyday concerns. Goals propel your relationship. They set a target point and put wind in your sails, enabling the relationship to travel to exciting new shores. Goals add the dynamic of purpose—a vitamin boost that enhances the vigor of your relationship.

Maybe you want to help eliminate world hunger, inspire people to go green, reduce pollution, elect a political candidate, reduce illiteracy, train as a marathon runner, become fluent in a new language, learn to hybridize orchids, become an antique furniture expert, start your own business, or return to school for an advanced degree.

The possibilities for exciting goals are endless. Finding the one (or ones) for you is a matter of searching your heart and mind to discover your personal dreams and examining the world around you to discover what's wanted and needed and how you might contribute.

THE VARIETY OF GOALS

Goals come in two varieties: those that you both share and those that only one of you pursues. Most writing on the subject emphasizes the importance of couples having common goals and overlooks the great value to a relationship of each partner having and pursuing his or her own separate ones, providing that the other partner accepts them as desirable and legitimate. We call the first kind **shared goals**, the second **agreed-upon goals**.

If you review the hypothetical list of goals mentioned earlier, you will see that each of them could be a shared goal or an agreed-upon goal. Maybe you will both take up running, maybe only one of you will. Maybe she starts learning a new language, and at a later date he decides to join her. Goals can be shared now, shared later, or belong to just one of you and supported by your partner. Any way you include them in your relationship adds purpose to your lives and lifts your relationship to another level.

Shared Goals

Some examples of couples with shared goals follow.

Dave and Lauren returned from a vacation with the recipe for a delicious sauce. They saw so much potential for it as a product that they decided to create a small business manufacturing and distributing it. Lauren has perfected the formulation for large quantities while Dave has taken out a business license and identified a source for glass jars. They have created a name for the product and are researching distribution channels. They are both excited about this new business venture and look toward production within the next few months. Last year's boredom seems like ancient history to them now.

Besides their jobs, Larry and Yuko volunteer many hours together raising money for and helping at a homeless shelter. They feel very strongly that people living on the street ought to be given a warm bed and hot meals and helped with whatever problems that keep them from having a home. Larry and Yuko have been involved with the shelter for fourteen years, and this crusade is a central part of their lives. Larry says: "I enjoy thoroughly working with [the organization]. . . . All the people are great. And they do a lot of good." And, Yuko says, "This work makes our lives seem worthwhile."

For us, a rewarding shared goal has been the creation of this book and its related training program for couples. We share the writing—each doing drafts of different sections—and then edit each other's work. The chapter assignments and other tasks are written down and updated regularly on a chart pad, and each of us agrees to do different facets of the overall project. We can hardly remember the lack of direction we felt a few years back when Ralph left an organization he had served for twenty-eight years and I had just completed a major project with a non-profit organization. Neither of us knew what to do next. This ongoing, shared goal has added purpose and great satisfaction to our lives.

Most couples understand that shared goals are important building blocks of their relationship. Most couples expect to have shared goals.

However, sometimes one partner takes for granted that his or her vision has automatically become a shared goal, when in fact it hasn't. Or a goal may be clearly shared, but the steps to its achievement haven't been laid out. For this reason, it's important that goals be verbalized and discussed, so they can move from ambiguity to open agreement and so the two of you can work together to specify the process and identify who contributes what to the outcome.

Agreed-Upon Goals

What about a goal desired by only one partner? It becomes an agreed-upon goal and an important part of your relationship, if the other partner says, "Go for it! It's not for me, but I'll support you in your pursuit." With separate agreed-upon goals, each partner's individual growth is nourished, personal dreams are not abandoned, and the result can be satisfaction and enrichment for both.

One partner may realize that she has always dreamed of piloting an airplane and decide she'd like to learn how to fly. Her partner has no interest in flying but supports her goal by agreeing to the necessary budget provisions, accepting the time it takes her, encouraging her studies, and cheerleading her growing skill in the cockpit. This couple has an agreed-upon goal. Here are more examples:

> Ryan, a successful computer engineer, secretly dreamed of teaching history. After soul-searching and long discussions with his wife, Carol, they agreed that she would continue working while he returned to school and turned his history minor into a major so he could teach at the secondary level. Carol agreed to Ryan's goal and supported his achievement of it. Now that he has started teaching, they both feel more comfortable in their academic social circle than they did in the high-tech industry.

> Ian is a physician with a family practice, but his real passion is evolution. With his wife's agreement, he spends a month each year in the rain forests of Brazil or Mexico's Sonora Desert, studying wild orchids and rare snakes in their natural habitat, because they fascinate him as being among the most primitive, unevolved, but fairly accessible organisms in the world. Ian has published extensively, and although his wife has no interest in snakes or tropical jungles, she is proud that his passionate interests have brought him deep satisfaction and many honors.

An example of an agreed-upon goal in our own relationship was my (Patty's) interest in roses. For many years, I was intensely involved with the cultivation and exhibition of roses. I wanted to become as expert as possible and to succeed in capturing trophies at rose shows, both locally and around the country. I attended numerous meetings to learn about the latest varieties and growing techniques, made modifications in our backyard to enlarge the growing beds, and devoted many hours to the tasks and pleasures associated with rose cultivation. Although Ralph was only mildly interested in roses himself, he readily agreed to my pursuit of those goals. And I enjoyed my many rose-growing achievements as well as the process of reaching them.

Along the way, Ralph joined me in attending rose meetings and shows, dug holes for plants, helped with the winter pruning, and actually became an expert himself on rose practices, even getting occasional calls from his male friends asking for rose-growing advice! Still, this was my hobby, not his—and an example of the closeness and pleasures that can result from the goal of one partner who is thoroughly supported by the other.

Supporting your partner in reaching a goal that is important only to her or him nurtures your feelings of closeness as partners, nurtures your partner as she or he stretches to achieve those goals, and nurtures your own feelings of self-worth as a loving, supportive person. Both partners benefit from agreed-upon goals.

Developing goals with your partner—both shared goals and agreed-upon goals—is an important way to develop bonds of closeness, as well as to give freedom, direction, and meaning to your lives. To know that your partner is in concert with you in working toward a shared goal or is in full support regarding something that is important only to you makes you feel deeply cared about and deeply connected as a couple. When you recognize clearly the many ways that embracing goals propels you toward happiness, personal satisfaction, and an increased sense of togetherness, you will want to grab your own clipboard!

2

PILLAR 2

AVOIDING BLAME

We find fault with perfection itself.

—Blaise Pascal

When something goes wrong, all but the saints among us rush to blame somebody for it. And we are usually ready, just as quickly, with character-correcting advice that we hope will prevent future occurrences. Blame and correction: what fun!

"If you hadn't left the phone off the hook again, I wouldn't have missed that important call!"

"It's all your fault that the cat got out. . . . . Why won't you remember to shut the screen door!"

"How do you expect me to find the place if you leave the directions at home?"

Blame is common, yet this all-too-familiar human behavior should be seen as relationship cancer. It invades your relationship like a tumor, eating away at all you cherish in the relationship, devouring everything, until your relationship has been drained of its vitality, pleasures, and satisfactions. It is a devastating disease that kills relationships.

Though blame is ubiquitous in most relationships, this rapidly spreading disease must not be allowed to develop. If unchecked, it will destroy everything special in your relationship. Blame hurts your partner's feelings; damages love, caring, closeness, and cooperation; breeds anger, resentment, and contempt; and lowers your partner's self-esteem. Blame's cancerous growth decimates many marriages—and you should halt its growth at the earliest stage possible.

Since blame is so harmful, minimizing it is beneficial to all relationships, including our relationship with ourself. Luckily, there is a way. It is a combination of a new way of thinking about the bad things that happen to us in life and a new way of talking about them to whomever else is involved.

A new way to think about things we tend to blame someone else for is to separate the "culprit" from the consequences. First, realize that the culprit—whatever his or her shortcomings—meant no harm and was doing his or her best under the circumstances. Even though your partner forgot to hang up the phone, left the door ajar, or forgot the directions at home, he or she meant well, even if the results were upsetting. It is important to take a moment to find a bit of empathy for your partner's innocent intentions by remembering that we all are always trying to do our very best. (Aren't you? Then isn't she or he?) Then concentrate on the consequences. They are what happened. They are what upset you. You missed an important call; the cat got out; you'll have to find a map to get to your destination. The important thing is not to make the culprit feel miserable but to solve the problem and move on.

It doesn't matter if your partner "caused" the problem. The important factors are dealing effectively both with your upset and the problem— and keeping your partner in the game.

A new way to talk about the consequences—instead of blaming and correcting your partner—is to disclose how the consequences actually affect you and what feelings you have about those effects. This can be done through an **I-Message**, developed by Thomas Gordon, in which you talk about what is true for you.[6] For example, here are some potential I-Messages for the previous examples:

"When you leave the phone off the hook and I miss a call that might be important, I feel really frustrated and irritated!"

"When you leave the screen door open and the cat gets out, I get really anxious that something will happen to her. I feel compelled to stop what I'm doing to go find her, and that's annoying."

"Without knowing how to get where we're going and spending a lot of time driving around, I'm now feeling pretty anxious about being late."

These are all examples of I-Messages without blame. Such self-disclosure helps you handle your feelings of upset, helps you tell the other person the effects of his or her behavior without rubbing his or her nose in it, and helps you clear the way for no-fault resolution of the problem. I-Language is clear and powerful yet avoids blame. It allows you to get your message across without putting your partner through hell. (See chapter 8, "Changing Behaviors, Not Your Partner," for a fuller discussion about how to get your needs met through self-disclosure.)

BAD-OLD BLAME

Everyone experiences the impulse to blame. Many times it seems very real that the other person "caused" this problem for you. But there are three fundamental realities to recognize: your own response to the consequences of the situation is the real cause of your upset; your relationship is more important than a moral victory; and a good, strong I-Message makes it much more likely that your partner will want to respond to your predicament in a caring and helpful way.

Unfortunately, blame is an extremely attractive way to deal with the feelings of helplessness that envelope us when something goes wrong. Your partner has just done something, the impact of which has been very upsetting to you, so what can you do about it? Nothing. It has happened. You are stuck with it. Helplessness is an emotion with which most adults have great difficulty dealing.

A typical way people experience their helplessness or upset is by getting angry and then yelling out in blame: "Damn it! Why'd you do that?" To many of us, there is nothing more attractive at moments of helplessness than to blame the nearest likely culprit—the person we assign responsibility for our upset feelings. Many times this person happens to be our partner, whom we supposedly love.

Remember that no matter how upsetting your partner's behavior may be to you, if you have a generally good relationship, the chances are high (to say the least) that your partner did not deliberately set out to hurt you. Keeping this in mind may help you stay on an even keel when you search for some way to express your upset without adding the kerosene of blame to the fire.

Everyone hates to be blamed. Moreover, it doesn't build character, no matter what your parents might have thought. It simply makes the other person feel guilty and defensive, it damages his or her self-esteem, and it often creates a temporary upset between you that erodes closeness. When allowed free rein, blame can cause a tremendous amount of damage to any relationship, no matter how loving you once might have been.

BLAME'S SOCIAL COUSIN—PUBLIC CRITICISM

Blame's social cousin is **public criticism**—the nasty practice of criticizing one's partner publicly. This is both humiliating and a terrible breach of the marital trust.

> "Sorry about the mess in the kitchen," Helen says, "but Don, as usual, still hasn't fixed the broken dishwasher, to say nothing of the porch light or the car window. Why he can't seem to take care of these things in less than a year is beyond me."

> "You know Bob—the tightwad. He never wants to spend money on anything. I don't know how he expects us to live like this."

> "Well, face it. My wife's a lazy slob. All she does is sit around talking to her girlfriends all day. She never lifts a finger around the house."

Unfortunately, you often hear such unpleasant criticisms in social situations. If it is painful for bystanders to hear, how much more painful it must be for the denigrated spouse! And how are friends to react when one spouse criticizes the other in his or her hearing? It's awkward for everyone. It certainly doesn't make for good social relationships.

Yet we all have grievances with our partners from time to time, and they sometimes arise when we are in the company of our friends. Must we always pretend that nothing is wrong? To do so would be artificial and stifle the honesty that makes true friendship a gift to cherish. So what guidelines can we use when we are upset with our spouse and are in the company of friends?

Rule number one, don't blame or criticize—and that includes the use of sarcasm. These are never appropriate responses but are especially inappropriate in public. Blame and criticism in public cause the additional hurt of embarrassment and humiliation. If you have a grievance with your partner about something she or he does, what you want is helpful change, not a deeply wounded, embarrassed, and resentful spouse.

Rule number two, apologize sincerely if you forget rule number one and hope for forgiveness. It's not likely to come quickly.

If you want to share problems honestly but safely with trusted friends, a beneficial alternative is expressing how you are affected by the problem and how you feel about that rather than blaming your spouse. For example, you might say that you're embarrassed by the mess in the kitchen and frustrated that the dishwasher hasn't been fixed yet. This is a true statement of the facts that deals with your feelings about the consequences, not the culprit, and leaves your spouse's dignity intact. Or a husband might say, "My wife and I have different values about housekeeping. I wish the house always looked cleaned up and squared away, but Sally is much more interested in keeping up with her friends. Sometimes I have a hard time accepting that. I wish it were different." Again, these are your feelings about the consequences, not the culprit.

To be congruent with close friends about concerns you want to share, the first rule is to preserve your spouse's dignity (and your own) by avoiding criticism. As we've shown, this can be done by talking about the consequences of the situation and your feelings about those, without blame, rather than talking about your partner.

BANISHING BLAME

In trying to banish blame, it may be helpful to think back to a time when you were blamed for something you did. How did that make you feel? What impact did that blame have on your self-esteem? Did you feel understood by the other person? How did it impact your future behavior? How did it impact your sense of closeness? How long did it take you to get over the feelings you had about feeling blamed? It is important to think about this soberly and realize that your partner is likely to have similar reactions to your blameful messages. This may help you grasp the cancerous nature of blame. Even with these realizations, it is not easy to give up blame, and because of the emotional complexities in the marriage relationship, it may be very hard to eradicate this damaging habit with your partner. Nevertheless, it is a goal of high importance.

The Power of Observation

To move closer to that goal, the best process is one that may at first seem ineffective but that has great potency over time. It is the simple process of being "at observation" about your behavior. Being at observation means just that—to silently observe, note, and acknowledge when you are assigning blame. Don't blame yourself when you notice this—or if you do, observe that you have just blamed yourself! Simply observe your own behavior.

The process of becoming aware helps you move toward consciousness about your own behavior, and this eventually gives you the opportunity to be conscious of and to choose your behavior. The trick is to be able to get a handle on your blaming—to be able to short-circuit the blame before it gets out of your mouth. Being at observation over a period of time without trying to force yourself to change will give you this ability, which will eventually create the opportunity for choice: you will reach a point where you can see yourself about to blame your spouse, and you will be able to choose not to do so. You will be able to choose another way to communicate your feelings of anger, annoyance, helplessness, rage, and so on. You will no longer be the victim of your habit of blaming—and neither will your partner!

The Power of Reflection

Another helpful way to control blame comes from the process of reflecting on the emotions that most trigger your tendency to blame. For most people, these are emotions related to anger. It is helpful to recognize that in many cases, anger is a secondary emotion that masks other deeper feelings we are uncomfortable acknowledging. Somehow, it often seems easier or safer to get irritated or angry than to deal with underlying feelings such as helplessness, fear, sadness, or hurt. These are four of the hardest feelings for adults to deal with—or even to recognize. Yet recognizing and expressing these more fundamental feelings is often the key to avoiding anger and blame, as well as to enlisting the support or cooperation of your mate.

In our personal life, for many months, I (Patty) berated Ralph for coming home late for supper: "Why were you late? You are supposed to be home by 6:45. Why didn't you call when you knew you would be late?" Was this really about me being upset about having to eat dinner alone or about waiting for Ralph to join me later? Not really. Upon reflection, I realized it was a combination of two other things: the wish to be so compelling to Ralph that no emergency could ever make him stay at work later than 6:30 and my (irrational) fear that he had gotten into a car accident on the freeway.

If you get in touch with your feelings of sadness and fear, as I eventually did in this situation, you can see that what you might say to a partner coming home late would be very different. Rather than berating your partner for being an inconsiderate, tardy workaholic, your new awareness would enable you to reveal, for example, "I just feel hurt when you aren't home by 6:45. I wish you were so eager to see me that you'd drop everything to rush home," or "When you weren't home by 7:00 and you didn't call, I became really scared that something terrible happened to you on the freeway. I've really been worried about you."

These are messages of vulnerability, and vulnerability is an invitation to empathy and closeness. Expressing your vulnerable self, rather than your angry, blaming, pushing-away self, makes it much easier for your partner to respond caringly. (Ralph agreed to call whenever he knew he would be home late. Endearingly, he still starts those calls, now many years later, by saying, "Don't worry, babe, I'm not dead on the freeway!")

Awareness of your feelings of sadness, hurt, fear, and helplessness can help halt tendencies to blame and allow you to express feelings that may be more deeply meaningful. These feelings are often much easier for your partner to deal with caringly than blame. Blame fosters distance in relationships and doesn't promote closeness, caring, concern, or problem solving. It is most important that you quit singing songs of blame if you wish to create a world class marriage.

SPECIAL BLAME TEMPTATION

Be alert to a special hazard built into this book: the temptation to say things like, "Hey! I thought we were supposed to be avoiding blame around here—that sounded like blame to me!" or "That sure didn't sound like I-Language!" Those kinds of messages may seem natural and appealing, especially if both partners read this book and subscribe to its ideas. However, saying something like that is a way of using the book as a club. Such messages are disguised blame, beefed up with a dose of self-righteousness, and like any other blameful message, they are hurtful. Instead, pull yourself up by the socks, and turn the desire to blame into a clean, blame-free I-Message and say something like, "When you say that, I just feel hurt and criticized," or whatever fits the situation.

NONVERBAL BLAME

It is also important to realize that blame can be communicated nonverbally, even when the words you use are blame-free. Your tone of voice and facial expression can transform, "That's OK—forget about it," from easy forgiveness to disgusted reproach. "Fine!" can have many other meanings than fine, depending on the context, tone of voice, and body language. Therefore, as you work to eliminate blame from your I-Language, it is important to become conscious of the message you are sending with your tone of voice, facial expression, and body language, as well as your words.

Making the effort to root out blame in your marital relationship is enormously worthwhile, and it is equally worthwhile to do this in your relationship with yourself. Blame is a cancer to be eradicated in every relationship you value, and it's critically important to develop a blame-free relationship with yourself. Remember: blame doesn't create growth. Sixty years of research resulting from Carl Rogers's pioneering work in psychotherapy makes it clear that **empathy** and **acceptance** are the two most powerful ingredients that help people grow and deal with problems. Remember this as you talk to yourself about your own behavior. Like anyone else who withers from blame and grows with empathy and acceptance, you need to create a climate of safety for yourself within which you can nurture your own growth.

We strongly encourage you to become conscious of blame in its many manifestations and to work on reducing its place in your relationship. There may be no single more powerful way you can improve your relationship together than to eradicate this cancer from your lives.

3

PILLAR 3

UNDERSTANDING THE
NATURE OF BEHAVIOR

I reckon there's as much human nature in some folks as there is in others, if not more.

—Edward Noyes Westcott

Behavior, according to Webster's New International Dictionary, is "the way an organism acts, especially in response to a stimulus." Human behavior is what people say and do—what you can see, hear, touch, taste, and smell with your five sense organs. Here are two important insights about human behavior:

Insight 1: You can influence your partner's actual behaviors much more easily than you can influence what you interpret to be his or her traits, attitudes, characteristics, or motives, which are internal, private, and not directly accessible. The great significance of this is the realization that attempts to change your partner's character or attitude are probably doomed, not to mention irritating. However, attempts to change the behaviors can be very successful! For example, if you want a bouquet of red roses for your birthday, it's much easier to ask for them than to try to make your partner a more "thoughtful and considerate person" who would think of this himself. The fundamental principle is this: things go much better in a relationship when you minimize your assumptions about what's going on inside your partner (and your desire to change it) and respond instead to what you can see, hear, or physically feel. Behaviors are the key!

Insight 2: Your partner's behaviors—welcome or not—are attempts to meet some personal need, not evidence of superior or inferior moral character or of a desire to annoy you. Unless you married a sociopath, which is unlikely, your partner is not behaving badly when his or her behavior displeases you; your partner has simply chosen a means of meeting a need that interferes with one of your needs or is otherwise unacceptable to you. If your partner reaches across the sink for the glass while you are brushing your teeth, she's not trying to irritate you; she just wants a drink of water. Your partner isn't being "inconsiderate"; she is simply trying to get her needs met.

All behavior is goal-directed—always an attempt to meet some need. It can be very helpful to recall this at times when your partner's behavior is unacceptable to you. This enables you to confront the behavior without blame and to listen much more empathically, which greatly increases your chances for helpful, voluntary behavior change or a mutually acceptable solution for the future.

> Lucy complains that Megan doesn't call her from work regularly. Is Megan deliberately trying to hurt Lucy by not calling? Not likely. Most people in a close and caring relationship do not deliberately set out to hurt each other. Thus, Megan's not calling is more likely a reflection of her focus and preoccupation with what's going on at work or perhaps not wanting her colleagues at work to be privy to details about her home life.

We can only speculate about what motivates our partner's behavior unless we open a dialogue with a climate of safety that allows the confronted partner to communicate authentically about his or her needs.

> Danielle arrives home with news she can't wait to share with Bart. She enters the room, already excitedly telling him the big news. He waves his hand at her emphatically, giving a clear message to stop talking immedi-

ately. She is momentarily hurt. She had big news she wanted to share, and he didn't want to hear it.

Was he trying to hurt her? Absolutely not. He was on the telephone, engrossed in an important conversation, and didn't want to be interrupted. His behavior, waving at her to stop talking, was an attempt to keep her from interfering with his ability to hear the person on the telephone. This was a legitimate need that in no way was deliberately intended to hurt her.

She, too, had a legitimate need—to share her exciting news with him—and her attempt to do this was not intended to interfere with his needs. Once she recognized her behavior caused him a problem, she was no longer hurt by his behavior and was able to back off and hold the big news until later. After Bart finished the phone call, they easily patched up the breach: he offered, "Sorry for having waved you off, but I was on a really important call," to which she responded, "Oh, that's okay. I didn't realize you were on the line." Then she shared her news with him.

We cannot emphasize enough that loving partners do not deliberately do things to irritate each other. When you are hurt by your partner's behavior, it is easy to think she or he acted uncaringly and then to blame your partner. But this doesn't work very well. Blame begets defensiveness. It doesn't foster caring and cooperation.

Thinking about the totality of your experience with your partner may help you realize that the irritation was not intentionally caused. Once you are grounded in that reality, you are more likely to understand the need your partner was attempting to meet. Your irritation will lessen and your compassion will increase. You will be in a much better position to confront with caring and listen with open ears. This will enhance the likelihood of reaching a new understanding or solution that will prevent future problems.

A further, highly beneficial insight comes from recognizing that whatever upset you is created within you: the upset is not a direct result of your partner's behavior. Your partner has done A; you respond by creating (voluntarily or involuntarily), inside of yourself, the feeling B. Your feeling B may be quite different than someone else's response to that situation, but this in no way diminishes the importance of your feeling.

The value of recognizing the fact that your feelings are something you create inside of yourself is that it enables you to confront your partner in a self-revealing way, rather than with blame. By acknowledging that your response to your partner's behavior is uncomfortable, difficult, or painful in some way for you changes the entire tone of the confrontation. Rather than a blame session, the confrontation becomes an opportunity to share with your partner what is going on with you, which can open the door to better understanding and a mutually agreed-upon change in the future, in addition to unexpected closeness.

Remembering that all behavior is an attempt to meet some need helps you to unlock some of the mystery about your partner and enables you to confront undesirable behavior with compassion and with an emphasis on self-revelation. When your partner has done something that upsets you, your partner is not being difficult or hurtful. Your partner is just trying to get his or her needs met. A world class marriage is created through the process of communicating with each other sensitively and clearly so that you recognize and understand each other's needs and find solutions together that work for both of you.

4

PILLAR 4

USING POWER LISTENING

My wife says I never listen to her. At least I think that's what she said.

—Anonymous

If you want a world class marriage, it is essential that you listen to your partner. Listening opens the doors to understanding. Listening builds trust. Listening facilitates conflict resolution. Listening is the mother of closeness. Listening fuels relationship growth. Theologian Paul Tillich summarizes its importance by saying, "The first duty of love is to listen."

Listening is the most powerful thing you can do to encourage your partner to talk to you. If you talk all the time and seldom listen, you shouldn't be surprised if your partner doesn't say much. You can observe this phenomenon clearly in parents who maintain a constant stream of directives, corrections, advice, and criticisms to their children and who then complain to their friends that their kids never talk to them, although they talk willingly to peers. The simple reason is that their peers listen and don't hand out so much unwanted advice. If you want your partner to share intimately with you, be an attentive listener. If you want a close relationship, keep your ears open for business.

Hank reported that he didn't feel he should bring home his work problems to Brianna, because they were irrelevant to her life and he didn't want to burden her with them. In a private session while they were practicing listening skills, Hank was persuaded to talk about a complex problem he had dealing with a client, while Brianna was asked to simply listen to him. After the exercise, to Hank's surprise, Brianna said that she was extremely interested in hearing about Hank's problem and had previously felt cut off from that important part of his life. And a beaming Hank said, "I loved telling her!"

Did Brianna solve Hank's problem at work? No. But Brianna's attentive listening provided an opportunity for Hank to share his thoughts and feelings and perhaps to get some insight about them or some emotional release from them, but most of all, it brought them closer together as a couple.

After getting comfortable with simply staying still and listening while your partner talks, you can move toward hearing what your partner says at a deeper level by making it your goal not only to understand your partner's words, but also to understand the emotional meaning of what your partner says. In our highly intellectualized world, this important aspect of communication is sadly neglected, and the casualties of this neglect are empathy and closeness.

Empathy can be defined as seeing the world through your partner's eyes. For a moment, set aside your own thoughts, feelings, judgments, and solutions, and use your partner's words, tone of voice, and body language as the pathway to experiencing what he or she is experiencing as closely as possible. Empathy means understanding where your partner is coming from without trying to change him or her. Empathy takes practice to develop, but it is one of the most valuable and affirming gifts you can give to your partner.

With empathy, you know that "We won the game!" means not only that our team beat their opponents, but also that your partner is thrilled about it. The message isn't just that your partner's team won the game; it's how glorious that felt. Tasting how wonderful this victory feels to your partner is an important way to experience closeness together.

Listening for your partner's emotional meaning as well as his thoughts helps you to truly understand him and to give him the satisfaction of being truly understood. Empathic understanding greatly enriches your relationship, your intimacy, your sense of being "in it together," your sense of satisfaction, and even your ability to resolve conflicts.

THE PROFOUND IMPORTANCE OF EMPATHY

Empathy is the single most powerful ingredient for helping another person to grow and to be able to handle his or her problems. This was well documented more than forty years ago by Bernard Berenson and Robert Carkhuff and other researchers of counselor-client relationships, who found that successful therapists offer strong empathy to their clients because they realize its value in helping clients deal with difficult situations in their lives. In fact, these studies found that the single most beneficial thing a counselor can do to help clients grow is to show them that they are deeply and nonjudgmentally understood. Why should we want anything less in our marriage?

Therapists communicate understanding and empathy to their clients by offering feedback that demonstrates their understanding of the client's thoughts and feelings. For this reason, this listening skill has been called "**reflective listening**." It is also known as **empathic listening** and **active listening**.

A subtle problem with this form of listening is that it doesn't seem like you are doing very much to help. It doesn't feel like powerful support. Yet the data are absolutely clear that empathy is the single most powerful way to help someone deal with a problem. For this reason, we have come to call this skill "**power listening**" to emphasize the potency of this response.

When someone important to us is hurting, the natural tendency is to jump in and do something to fix the problem—offer solutions, ask questions, and give advice and constructive comments—anything that might benefit your partner and help him or her out of difficulty. But what happens when you try to offer advice and other forms of "help"? Usually these efforts are met with resistance—sometimes great resistance. In my (Ralph's) case, whenever I forget to listen and start making wise suggestions, Patty says, "Don't try to help, I just want you to listen to me!" As our colleague Speed Burch liked to say about such suggestions, "Help strikes again!"

Despite the fact that empathic listening (power listening) has been shown to be the single most powerful way to help someone deal with a problem, it is not always easy for the listener to resist the desire to do something more than "just listen." It takes discipline to resist jumping in with some of the more conventional ways of "helping," such as offering advice, asking questions, giving solutions, providing reassurance, and all the other approaches that feel common and "natural" but yet are far less effective. The problem is, when our partner has a problem, we sometimes then have a subtle problem ourselves. For many reasons, we prefer our partner to be trouble-free. When our partner is troubled, we feel helpless. To rid ourselves of that terrible feeling, we itch to do something: most especially, we itch to offer advice, solutions, almost any kind of "help," except what really works—accepting, empathic listening with feedback that demonstrates that we hear and understand what is going on in our partner. Our difficulty dealing with this helplessness is why "help"—so often—"strikes again!"

A good preventive tactic is acknowledging to your partner how helpless you feel when you hear about his or her problem ("I can barely sit here and listen to your problem without wanting to jump in and fix it for you!"). Expressing your feelings like this is likely to lessen your sense of helplessness, which makes it easier to offer your partner some real help—by power listening to his or her thoughts and feelings.

THE NATURE OF FEELINGS

Feelings are not rational. They come unbidden, and they don't follow the rules of logic. They are just there. They are our organic, visceral responses to whatever is going on in our environment, internal and external. Our thoughts do not control them. They are our wants, our desires, our needs, our fears, our sorrows, our joys. Feelings often motivate goal-seeking behaviors; our stated reasons are often just our conscious mind's rationalizations for doing what our emotions want us to do. So when feelings are aroused, there's no use in trying to be logical or rational until the feelings have been experienced, accepted, and allowed to pass.

And they do pass. Feelings, by their nature, are transitory. They come and go. However painful, joyful, or even mundane your feelings may be, none of them lasts forever. Their nature is to change, with new ones supplanting the old in a neverending continuum.

The exceptions are feelings we do not allow ourselves to experience—the ones we block or suppress because they are too scary, overwhelming, or seemingly unacceptable for us to acknowledge or share. We tell ourselves, "I suppose this is upsetting, but I don't want to dwell on it." Or, "I just don't want to deal with it." Or, "C'mon, put on a happy face!" Or, "I'm too embarrassed to tell anyone how I really feel."

When we do this, such feelings retain their hold on us, making us unhappy, depressed, or angry, sometimes for long periods, and this can interfere with our ability to cope rationally with the problem that caused them. By offering power listening, you can prevent this from happening to your spouse. If you offer a safe, empathic ear—without criticism, questions, or advice—whenever she or he is troubled or upset, your listening will help your partner to explore the problem and express and accept the darkest of feelings so that they loosen their grip and your partner can face and experience them. And they will move on.

By the same token, the most helpful posture to take in regard to your own feelings is to be open to experiencing them, whatever they may be. It is greatly beneficial for us to be in touch with our feelings. It enables us to experience the joys in our lives and to get relief from our pain. And the greatest help we can receive in actualizing an open posture toward our feelings is to have our loving partner listen to us.

We encourage you to do what you can within yourself to have an open posture toward your feelings, to adopt the position that feelings are to be welcomed into your conscious life, whether they make sense to you or not. When you open the door to your own feelings, listening to them within yourself, allowing whatever feelings there may be to exist without censoring or labeling them as good or bad, you open the door into a richer life. As you admit into your own consciousness a greater array of emotions, it becomes easier for you to listen to your partner's feelings, offering your partner the chance to be a fuller human being as well. Your relationship is enriched by this depth; it helps you achieve the deepest degree of intimacy together.

LISTENING SKILLS

There are several types of listening skills, ranging from simple behaviors to complex ones. The most basic listening skill is simply to invite your partner to talk, then listen. When you notice that she or he seems upset or worried or angry or excited—in other words, when she or he seems to be experiencing something emotionally—open the door for your partner to talk about it. This is very easily and naturally done: "Wow, what's happened?" "Is there something you'd like to talk about?" "How'd it work out today?" "You look pleased with yourself. Want to tell me about it?" When you invite your partner to talk, it helps start this process.

Then shut your mouth and give your partner the opportunity to use the airspace. This works surprisingly well. Despite how simple it is to give this to your partner, many adults in our workshops report that they have never in their lives been given this much freedom to talk. Most people are so eager to express themselves that they never give their partner uninterrupted airspace. This can be a meaningful gift. Silence and attention convey respect and caring, and silence creates the opportunity for your partner to share his or her thoughts and feelings with you. If you want your partner to open up to you, this is essential.

Besides simply not interrupting, "be with" your partner. Focus your full attention on her or him and do your best to avoid distractions, like thinking about what advice you should give. When you intend to attend, it is simple to do and very powerful.

Your body language is an important part of attending. It not only conveys your attention to the speaker, but also increases your ability to focus. Good body language includes facing your partner, on the same eye level, with a receptive expression on your face, making good eye contact, and leaning slightly toward the other, avoiding a closed posture of folded arms and crossed legs.

Another simple way to encourage meaningful communication with your partner is to make normal, quasi-verbal responses to what your partner is saying. These are sometimes referred to as "empathic grunts" or "noncommittal acknowledgments," which are simple words and utterances that communicate that you are hearing and relating to what's being said, that you are engaged in the conversation without intending to interfere with it, and that you are still interested in listening. Such responses encourage your partner to continue talking. Examples are "uh-huh," "oh," "wow!" "really!" "I understand," "oh, my goodness!" "gee!" and the classic "Mmmm." These, supplemented with empathic nods of the head, are simple and natural ways to encourage the flow of communication from your partner.

These passive forms of listening (what we call **power listening lite**) help your partner talk about whatever is on his or her mind—safe from your judgments, advice, and probing questions. They communicate your interest and caring and facilitate communication. These are beneficial, relationship-enhancing skills that can be employed successfully immediately. All it takes is your doing so.

THE DEEPEST LISTENING

Although many people have heard of empathic listening, few use it when it matters most. Power listening is so powerful and beneficial to relationships that we strongly encourage you to make a full commitment to learning and using this skill if you want to have a world class marriage. You may also seek additional reinforcement from a marriage education or relationship education class. (Courses are taught nationwide through community Healthy Marriage initiatives, faith-based organizations, community colleges, university extensions, YMCAs, and training institutes.)

Power listening is listening royalty. More strongly than any other, this skill communicates understanding and empathy, and it allows your partner to express his or her thoughts and feelings, to release the emotions that grip him or her, and to find a resolution to the problem. Power listening is a skill that professional counselors and therapists use in their practices because it is the most powerful way to help someone deal with their personal problems. Power listening consists of understanding the meaning of your partner's message clearly enough that you can accurately summarize it.

To do this when your partner talks about a problem, pay special attention to what your partner is feeling as well as her thoughts. The feelings may be expressed verbally or nonverbally. When you grasp your partner's message—both feelings and thoughts—put this into your own words. For example, after your partner angrily tells you about an un-reasonable reprimand from a supervisor, you might respond by saying, "It really ticks you off when he acts like that!" After a description of an interminable wait at the doctor's office, you might say, "How frustrating to spend so much time waiting!" After hearing your partner complain about clothing, you might say, "You just hate it when you don't have anything you think you look good in!" After your partner describes being overlooked for a raise, you might say, "It's very painful and frustrating to feel that your contributions are not recognized and appreciated."

There are many ways to feed back the above examples. There are no perfect feedbacks, only your best guess, given the cues you receive. The key is to ask yourself, "What is the gist of what my partner is saying?"

GETTING THE GIST

To be an empathic listener, you need to focus on getting the **gist** of your partner's message and feeding that back. That is why the skill is some-times referred to as "reflective listening," because you attempt to reflect back to your partner the gist of what you hear as his or her message.

It's not difficult to get the meaning of what your partner is saying. Most people have a strong sense of the gist of every message they hear. What's new here is summarizing it for your partner so that she knows you have heard and understood her and so that she gets to hear it again for herself. This gives her a clearer understanding of her own thoughts and often a release from troublesome feelings, which makes it easier for her to explore the problem and find her own solutions. Furthermore, it provides the deep satisfaction that arises from the knowledge that the person she cares most about really knows how she feels.

Do not underestimate how much this means to your partner. For some reason, most human beings strongly want their partner to under-stand their feelings about the important things in their lives.

If you have trouble getting the gist of your partner's message, ask yourself these questions:

What is my partner feeling?
What is my partner thinking?
What is it like to be my partner in this situation?

What is the message she or he wants me to hear?
What would I be feeling if I talked this way?

Remember, there are no perfect feedbacks, only your best guess given the cues you receive. Get into your partner's shoes and see the situation through his or her eyes. It doesn't matter whether it makes sense to you, whether you would feel that way, or how you would handle the situation. Just grasp how it is for your partner and reflect that back in your feedbacks, offered at the times when your partner pauses in his or her communication.

If your feedback of the message is accurate, your partner will acknowledge this, and if it is a complex matter, continue to talk about the subject by moving on to another aspect of it. Again, after listening for a while, summarize the gist of the next group of thoughts and feelings and feed this back. A brief "yes" and continued exploration of the matter will likely follow, until the subject runs its course. This happens naturally, and you know you're at the end of the exchange when your partner runs out of emotional steam, seems calmer, says she or he feels better, or simply changes the subject.

Often your partner will thank you for listening. Sometimes "just listening" doesn't feel as if you've done much, but keep in mind all the studies that have shown how invaluable this is.

To this we add, power listening is also appropriate to relationship building when your partner is experiencing a sense of happiness or success. One of the loveliest joys of a world class marriage is sharing with your partner the deliciousness of a hard-won victory and knowing that your partner really understands what a wonderful feeling that is for you. Imagine if you'd finished first in a marathon and your partner didn't fully comprehend the huge sense of accomplishment you felt. But if she or he really hears your exaltation and feeds it back with joy, the pleasures of sharing your sense of triumph and happiness with your partner adds meaning to the triumph and closeness to your relationship.

WHY SKILLED LISTENING IS IMPORTANT

When you talk to people about something troubling, many times they say, "I hear you," "I understand," "I know how you feel," "I've been there, too," and other similar attempts at empathy. Unfortunately, these weak attempts don't do the job. You could say such a thing even if you hadn't listened to one word the other person said. These responses sound good but they may be hollow. What human beings want is to know that their partner truly understands them.

Power listening is proof positive that you understand. This is what we crave, and power listening delivers the goods. When you accurately feed back your partner's message, she or he will feel understood, because she or he will know beyond any doubt, through the words you use in your feedback and your tone of voice and other body language, that you truly understand.

This caring feedback, based in empathy and acceptance, is what helps release the difficult feelings, unscramble the confused thoughts, and clear the path for new solutions. It's a drug-free miracle cure. Because power listening communicates both empathy and acceptance, it supplies the two most powerful ingredients that help someone deal with problems and it plays an essential role in developing a close and caring relationship.

The role of listening is summed up well by the writer George Eliot who said, "We want people to feel with us more than to act for us." When we are struggling with frustration, discouragement, confusion, hurt, sadness, or pain of any kind, we want people—especially our spouse—to listen to and empathize with our thoughts and feelings, not to try to solve our problem for us. Everyone wants to feel understood, and we most especially want this from our partner. It is the empathy and acceptance of power listening that helps people grow and develop the capacity to deal with life's problems and simultaneously nurture the bonds of their relationship. No world class marriage is without it.

(5)

PILLAR 5

GIVING UP "TIT FOR TAT"

"When Your Phone Don't Ring (It'll Be Me)"

—Country-western hit recorded by George Jones

You and your partner are both on a diet and avoiding sweets. After dinner in a restaurant, your partner orders a slice of chocolate cake à la mode. You say, "Well, if you're going off your diet tonight, I will, too."

Your partner has been making you upset by flirting at parties you go to. You announce you've decided to do the same, and say, "We'll see how the shoe fits when it's on the other foot!"

You are the only one who picks up the little messes of daily living around the house. Finally you blurt out, "I'm sick of being the only one who cleans up around here; it's your turn now!"

These are examples of "**tit for tat**." They communicate, "If you can do it, I can do it"; "If you hurt me, I get to hurt you"; "If I do it for you, you must do it for me." Get the idea? It's the same thinking that produced sayings like, "What's good for the goose is good for the gander," "A blow for a blow," or "An eye for an eye and a tooth for a tooth."

The trouble is, there's a terrible flaw in the logic. It's an attempt to attribute cause and effect where there is only correlation. Worse yet—and herein lies its attractiveness—it allows you to meet your needs without taking responsibility for them.

In the first example, you pretend that your partner's diet lapse causes, or at least justifies, yours. In the second, you are pretending to be justified in punishing your partner for his or her flirtatious behavior with similar behavior. In the third, you manipulate with guilt disguised as fairness to force your partner to help you around the house. The irresponsibility of these tactics is almost obscured by the nearly universal acceptance of tit for tat's validity. It is widely practiced, but a policy of an eye for an eye and a tooth for a tooth in your marriage results in two one-eyed, gap-toothed partners in a miserable relationship.

When the temptation to use tit for tat arises, it's best to stop and examine your needs and motives. Having dessert because your partner does is a way to use your partner's behavior to justify doing what you want to do without taking responsibility for it. In fact, if that ploy goes unchallenged, you can later blame your partner if you gain a few pounds! This kind of polluted thinking is bad for relationships. A far better approach is to admit to yourself that you want dessert, even though it's forbidden on your diet. Then decide if you are willing to put up with the resulting added weight and the little nick in your motivation to stick to your diet. If you then decide to order the chocolate cake, you have made a responsible decision based on the considerations rather than putting the responsibility onto your partner.

The flirtation example entails two components that avoid responsibility. If what you really want to do is carry on flirtations, you need to acknowledge that to yourself and consider the many consequences of such a decision. The other form of irresponsibility is using your behavior as a way to punish your partner for hurting you and using his or her behavior as a justification for your behavior and as a shield against his or her disapproval. Two wrongs don't make a right. (And three wrongs don't make a right either!) It is far better to have the courage to confront him or her clearly and congruently by explaining how hurt and anxious his or her flirting makes you feel, listening to his or her side of the story, and working it out between you, than to sully your precious relationship with any version of tit for tat.

With the housework example, if you want help in keeping the house tidy, ask for it. Don't demean yourself by using fairness as a weapon with which to manipulate your beloved. If help is not then forthcoming, you have a conflict that must be resolved in some creative way that meets your needs as well as your partner's. Problem solving is much kinder to the relationship than a dose of tit for tat.

When your partner has done something upsetting or hurtful to you, it is important to communicate that, first by confronting (without blame), and then by listening to your partner's response to your confrontation. The result of this may be that your hurt feelings are resolved and your partner changes his or her behavior. Or you may find that you have a conflict that you need to work out together in a way that is acceptable to both of you. In either case, with confronting, listening, and problem solving, closeness can replace hurt, and solutions can be found that meet both of your needs. Tit for tat never results in such outcomes.

VERBAL TIT FOR TAT

For many couples, tit for tat is played out verbally and isn't connected with any other behavior. But verbal tit for tat can have surprisingly hurtful results.

> Samantha says, "I had a miserable time trying to sleep last night because of all your coughing." Ivan responds, "Well, it was no picnic for me having to listen to your snoring."

Verbal tit for tat: you say something blameful, critical, or scolding to me, and I return the same to you.

> Ben says, "What's the point of being on time—you're always late." Randy shoots back, "Yeah, but at least I answer my cell phone—unlike you!"

> Trevor says, "Why should I bother working out—you're a bigger slob than I am." Becky retorts, "Maybe I would care if you looked at me anymore."

This verbal fencing works just like the sport of fencing. You thrust; your partner parries. Touché! Touché! But unlike the sport of fencing, there are always two losers to the game of verbal tit for tat. It is a quick and dirty manifestation of the blame game—and as we have already discussed, there is nothing more corrosive to a relationship than blame.

However, a closer inspection of what's being said in these verbal volleys reveals valuable information about what each partner is feeling and thinking. The problem is that these important data are being used as swords to wound the partner when in fact they are valuable, emotion-filled communications that should be dealt with in a sensitive and careful way. However, their use as weapons to wound the partner precludes them from being dealt with and resolved effectively.

The way to short-circuit verbal tit for tat is to stop it at round 1. This isn't easy to do, but it is essential. When you hear a criticism from your partner—no matter how slight or sharp, *stop* yourself before flying back at your partner with a verbal tit for tat, calm yourself to the extent you can, and gather yourself in preparation to power listen to your partner's response to your original message.

In the previous examples, appropriate power listening responses might be:

> "It sure sounds like my coughing was very disturbing and annoying to you last night."

> "It sounds like my being late is a very annoying habit for you to deal with."

> "It sounds like you've really become disturbed by the way I look."

When you stop to power listen to your partner's criticism, you open the door to a serious and important dialogue about a problem that may have been festering in your relationship. The problem was raised somehow from this situation, perhaps in a way in which your partner never anticipated discussing, but it nevertheless is a problem that has been annoying to your partner, bearing serious discussion and begging for a satisfying solution.

When you power listen to your partner's initial foray into this discussion—however blameful it may have been—it eliminates verbal fencing, slows the discussion down, and brings it into a blame-free frame of reference. This opens the door for a meaningful discussion.

For example, in the previous situations:

"Well, yes, it really did bother me to hear you hacking away, and I was upset about losing so much sleep before such a big day at work today."

"Yes, it really is. I wish I could count on you being on time. I'd really like that."

"Yes. I really hate to see you looking so bad. I married a beautiful woman, and it's terrible for me not to have that anymore."

It's evident at this point that you and your partner have begun a truly intimate discussion about an important issue in your lives together. The dialogue is deep, the problem is a real one, and now you are facing it together in an open and honest way. The relationship can be enhanced by this quality of communication and perhaps also by an eventual solution to the problem.

None of this can happen if you respond to the initial volley with a verbal tit for tat. Instead of the intimate dialogue that can be created by power listening, your verbal tit for tat escalates your partner's critical comment into a situation where both of you take blows.

As your mother always said, "Two wrongs don't make a right," and no relationship thrives with verbal tit for tat. Insults and attacks don't create intimacy, and they don't open the door to satisfying solutions. When you hear your partner say something critical about you, try not to take it as an attack, resist being defensive, and reorient your response to a productive one by power listening to the genuine concern that lies behind your partner's comment. Transform the temptation for a touché into the opportunity for emotional touching.

COERCED RECIPROCATION: A SUBTLE VARIATION

Drew says to Diana, "I'm always giving you back rubs, but you never offer to give me one. I think you owe me."

Drew is trying to get Diana to reciprocate his generosity with a back rub from her. Because Drew has given her many, he thinks he's entitled to get some from her and is trying to pressure her to reciprocate out of a sense of fairness (a seemingly "positive" tit for tat.) Unfortunately, this is a formula for taking a generous act and turning it into **coerced reciprocation**. This version of tit for tat doesn't work, either. Doing something nice for you does not obligate you to do something nice for me, unless the two of us have previously made such a deal. Gifts are gifts, whatever the gift may be. If there are strings attached, they are not gifts. If you want a back rub, ask for one. Don't try to corner your partner by adding coercion, "After all, I give you a lot of back rubs, so you should give me some, too." Your partner needs to be given the opportunity to respond to a request with a free heart.

Generally, unless your need is imperative, it is beneficial if you are open to either a "yes" or "no" answer when you make a request, whether it's about bringing you a glass of water, going to a ball game together, or having sex. Ironically, when given the freedom to decide to do (or not to do) something you request, your partner is more likely to be willing to give it. And, wonderfully, the exchange does not get polluted with the dynamic of obligation.

The bottom line is that tit for tat in any of its manifestations is a deceptively fair-looking way to be grossly unfair. Recognize that you are separate people, with your own needs. Take responsibility for your own behavior without using your partner's behavior to justify it; ask your partner for what you want without using "fairness" as a weapon to coerce it; and never use tit for tat for retaliation when what is needed is direct, congruent confrontation. Always have the courage to make your own needs known and pursue them directly rather than using tit for tat as a crutch.

6

PILLAR 6

ASSUMING SELF-RESPONSIBILITY

Take life in your own hands, and what happens? A terrible thing: No one to blame.

—Erica Jong

Everyone is familiar with the concept of taking responsibility for his or her own behavior. This is an important precept of being a mature human being.

The corresponding concept in a relationship is the importance of taking responsibility for getting your needs met as a human being. It is up to you to see that this is done. You are the one responsible for yourself—for identifying your needs, hopes, and aspirations for your life, for following your dreams, and for making them happen for yourself.

Although a loving partner is likely to want to help you in getting those needs met, it is not your partner's responsibility to see that this happens. Your partner does this for you if and when she or he can, and it is always a voluntary matter. To expect your partner to be responsible for meeting your needs is to place too heavy a burden on another human being, no matter how much this human being may love you.

Taking responsibility for yourself can be mundane or profound. In our relationship, I (Patty) was frustrated with the way Ralph handled hotel check-ins. After talking with the desk clerk, Ralph would happily announce to me that we had a room, but when I asked about the room ("How much?"; "What size bed?"; "Is there a view?"; etc.), he often had no answer to those questions. This confounded and annoyed me, and I found it difficult not to be blameful ("You didn't even ask how much?").

Over several nights of discussion about this on our vacation, I came to realize that Ralph didn't particularly care about the cost, the size of the bed, or the view—those were my needs alone. I realized that if I wished to have the answers to those questions, I needed to take responsibility for making sure those questions were asked prior to checking in. We decided that I would handle hotel check-ins, which I have done ever since. I am able to get my information needs met prior to booking the room, and Ralph is happy not to have to handle the procedure. The solution works for both of us now that I am conscious of my own needs and willing to take responsibility for getting them met.

Although this example may seem mundane and may not immediately come to mind as an example of "taking responsibility for your life," it illustrates the importance of taking responsibility for your own needs in day-to-day situations.

> After several years of watching Roberto's diabetic complications gradually degrade his health, Sandra realized that she could not count on him to secure her financial future. She went back to school, got a teaching credential, and started teaching at a local high school. This additional income is enjoyed by their family now, and it will mean that the family will be financially secure should Roberto's health problems force his early retirement.

> After several years of yearning for things they couldn't afford and frustration with her husband's poor income, Dawn has taken over from Manny the management of their investments. Starting with a small amount of money, she has spent time learning how to invest in the stock market, and she follows their investments carefully every day. Rather than feeling frustrated that Manny's salary isn't enough to pay for the extras in life that she wants or complaining or criticizing, Dawn has taken responsibility for developing her capacity to maximize their money through profitable investments. She finds the process fascinating, has expanded her knowledge

about many related subjects, and has a powerful sense of being in control of her own fate. She shares the progress of their stocks with Manny on a regular basis, and this has become an exciting new development in their relationship.

These examples illustrate a process in which one of the partners woke up to realize an unmet need and made the decision to take responsibility for it. In doing so, they made a healthy shift in removing responsibility from their partner and accepting it for themselves. Sometimes, this is all that is necessary to create a transformation in your life and in your relationship.

RECOGNIZING UNMET NEEDS

Hearing herself say, "You didn't even find out how much the room cost?" was a wake-up call to Patty in recognizing and dealing with an unmet need. Feelings of resentment or a tone of irritation or frustration can be a tip-off that your needs aren't being met. If you hear resentment, criticism, or frustration in your words or in your voice when talking about your situation, your dreams, or your goals, it is a sign that you have some unmet need you should address. This is an opportunity for meaningful communication that can open the door to a new agreed-upon goal or a new decision or solution, adding greater strength and meaning to your relationship.

Paradoxically, sharing the realization with your partner that you recognize that this issue is *your* responsibility and not his or hers may generate your partner's interest in helping you to reach that goal—whether that goal is financial security, information, beauty, rest, stimulation, learning, safety, or whatever it may be—simply because you have fully assumed responsibility.

One of the great challenges in life is identifying who you are, who you wish to be, how you wish to spend your time on this planet, how you wish to interact with the world, and what things are important to you. This represents the essence of each person's life task—to be the person you wish to be. Recognizing the primacy of taking responsibility for your own life empowers you as an individual and enhances your sense of competence and satisfaction. And, most wonderfully, being able to own responsibility for your needs erases the burden of inappropriate expectations from your partner, frees you to meet your own needs, and, in general, allows you both the pleasure of voluntarily contributing to the other's life with a willing heart.

(7)

PILLAR 7

AVOIDING "COOL" TALK

Sarcasm is just one more service we offer.

—Anonymous

Today's popular jargon spread by television sitcoms, rap recordings, and Internet chat rooms tends to be cool, detached, ironic, and often somewhat hostile. It's catchy and it can be fun to sprinkle what you say with popular expressions and ironic comments like, "Yeah, right!" or "He's a real brain—Not!" or "Whatever."

But whenever feelings are at stake, irony, sarcasm, catchphrases, and other types of **"cool" talk** tend to be unclear and are dangerous forms of communication that leave room for misinterpretation and hurt. When emotions are aroused, any message other than a straightforward statement of your honest thoughts and feelings entails the risk of misunderstanding, confusion, or pain.

Irony—saying the opposite of what you mean to create an amusing effect—is fun in small doses and when feelings are not raw. But using irony as a primary way of relating to your partner comes across as being detached rather than engaged and vulnerable. It's cool, in the emotional sense; the opposite of warm and loving. Cool doesn't generate warm and loving relationships, so use it sparingly.

Sarcasm—irony that is sneering or cutting—is almost always hurtful. Its use creates nicks and dings in the partner's feelings, erodes confidence and self-esteem, and has no place in a world class marriage.

Current expressions that are "cool" are also sometimes hostile and often without clear meaning. For example, "Gimme a break!" may seem like a cool, safe way to say, "That's a dumb idea!" but it's less than a clear, self-revealing message. It leaves your partner with the vague feeling of having said or done something wrong, but not having a clear idea as to what, why, or how, and makes it risky for him or her to ask. The exchange can quickly shut down communication and end up hurting your partner's feelings and putting distance between you.

It's important to remember that characters on a television sitcom use sarcasm, irony, and other forms of indirect communication because they are supposed to sound cool and play for laughs, no matter how painful these messages are to other characters in the show. They are also supposed to set up misunderstandings to thicken the plot. They don't care how much confusion and hurt they cause because their job is to entertain the audience, not to create a genuinely close and loving relationship. With your loved one, you have different goals, and you're much more likely to succeed if you communicate clearly, openly, and directly. When the chips are down, cool talk isn't cool. It can be playful and fun when used in small doses but keep in mind that cool talk is always cool, and what you're looking to create with your partner is warmth.

8

PILLAR 8

CHANGING BEHAVIORS, NOT YOUR PARTNER

I dated this girl for two years—and then the nagging starts: "I wanna know your name."

—Mike Binder

In a word, you can't change your partner. Your partner is a separate human being, entitled to be who he or she is. Continual attempts to change foster resentment and even entrenchment of behaviors and traits you don't like. Most attempts to change a partner's character are doomed from the start. Adults don't change much.

Take a classic case of misplaced optimism: a girl falls in love with a handsome, charming, sexy hunk who drinks and gambles and loves the ladies too well. She's attracted to him for all his exciting qualities and promises herself that she can domesticate him and turn him into the perfect partner. When the honeymoon is over, she finds to her sorrow that try as she may, he continues to be all the things he was, the good and the bad.

Your best defense against such a disaster, of course, is to choose a partner whose character is a better match for yours.

Assuming that is the course you have followed, even the most careful singles generally realize sometime after the honeymoon that they have hooked up with someone who has a sprinkling of characteristics they wish were different.

So what can you do?

THE IMPORTANCE OF ACCEPTANCE

First, notice that your partner is a whole, complex human being with a huge repertoire of characteristics and behaviors, most of which you like and none of which you can prune off with a pair of scissors. Your partner is a package deal. It's best, as the song says, to accentuate the positive. Recognize what a great package you've bought and put your complaints in perspective. In short, develop acceptance.

Counseling research has clearly shown that by providing a climate of acceptance, where the other person feels safe to be who she or he is without fear of criticism, he or she can experience amazing growth and change. Over the years of your life together, your acceptance of your partner can nourish similar growth and change. Note that while the direction the growth takes is chosen by your partner, not you, all growth tends to produce a richer human being for you to relate to.

Ironically, genuine acceptance sometimes opens the door to change, even on specific issues, whereas direct attempts to change bring resistance. This is a powerful but puzzling dynamic. This puzzlement is resolved by realizing that when you push, the other guy usually pushes back. What you resist, persists. In other words, pressure to change acts in a paradoxical way to create resistance to that pressure. Parents of teenagers know this, sometimes too well, but it's just as true for adults.

Courtney's husband, Bob, continually nagged her to lose weight. Courtney responded by maintaining she was only pleasingly plump and told Bob to get off her back. Finally, Bob gave up. You know the rest of the story: once Bob quit badgering her to lose weight, Courtney was free to make her own decision about her size and eventually the extra weight was gone.

Serena and Ken lived together as an unmarried couple for five years, most of those years with Serena pestering Ken to get married. He continually resisted, saying, "someday." Serena was frustrated; Ken felt cornered. Finally Serena realized she wasn't getting anywhere by nagging and decided to make peace with herself by recognizing that even though they weren't married they otherwise had a good relationship that she really enjoyed, and she stopped pressuring Ken into marriage. You know the rest of this story, too: a few months later Ken proposed and Serena got her wish after all.

In our own relationship, I, Patty, know personally the long-term power of acceptance, because this is one of Ralph's strongest characteristics. I have basked in the sunshine of it for many years. As a result, I have grown to be a stronger and happier person—more accepting of others, more accepting of myself, and more confident in my ability to tackle problems in my life—and a more developed, more satisfying human being for Ralph to be married to.

CHANGING BEHAVIORS THAT BOTHER YOU

Sometimes, your partner's behaviors are not acceptable to you. Thankfully, as we noted in chapter 3, "Understanding the Nature of Behavior," your partner's behaviors—what they do or say—are much more amenable to change than character traits or attitudes.

Your husband walks on the carpet with shoes still muddy from working in the garden.

Your wife criticizes you sharply for failing to pay a bill on time.

Your partner spends the grocery money on lottery tickets.

Your partner forgets your birthday—no gift, no card, no celebration.

Your mate hogs the television remote, usually watching programs you have no interest in.

When our partner's behavior upsets us, our first reaction tends to be modeled on how our parents corrected our behavior when we upset them—usually with blame, directives, or moralizing. "You clean that up right this minute!" "How could you be so careless?" "I can't believe you gambled with the grocery money!" "Don't you ever think of anybody but yourself?" "Don't you even care what I'd like to watch?" These tendencies are registered deep within us and get activated very quickly when our partner unexpectedly does something that's upsetting.

If we succumb to these blameful old echoes, our partner's response will usually be similar to how she or he reacted to this type of confrontation with her or his parents—resisting, arguing, or pouting. This is not the sort of interaction that fosters a world class marriage between two adults. How can we handle behavior we don't like in a healthier way?

The first step is to remember that categorizing your partner's behavior as an attitude or characteristic—insensitive, selfish, careless, inconsiderate, lazy, stupid, immoral, rude, and so forth—simply hurts your partner's feelings and creates anger and resistance. And barking orders like a stern parent adds to it.

What works much better is remembering that you are in a caring relationship and that your partner would never hurt you on purpose. That grounding helps you short-circuit the desire to blame. Then you can realize that your partner must not have known, or somehow did not realize, the negative effect his behavior had on you. The remedy, of course, is to tell him—share the effects on you of his behavior and trust that she or he will take positive steps to remedy the situation.

> "Oh, Frank! The carpet's getting all muddy. I'm afraid it's going to get badly stained, and we'll have to pay to get it cleaned."

> "Ouch! It feels terrible to have upset you. And I guess it feels even worse because I was already berating myself for being stupid. I'm really feeling bad."

> "Wesley, when money I counted on to buy food gets spent on something else, I feel shocked and really panicky, not knowing what else we'll have to sacrifice to be able to pay for this week's groceries."

> "Having my birthday forgotten makes me feel so unimportant and uncared about. I can't tell you how sad I feel."

"When you control the remote and choose all the programs, I miss ones I like and end up watching stuff I'm not interested in or doing something else, and I'm beginning to feel resentful about that."

These messages use I-Language, as opposed to You-Language: I describe what's happening to me rather than what's wrong with you. These messages have two important characteristics. First, they don't criticize your partner. Second, they tell your partner very clearly what his or her behavior means to you in terms of your needs and feelings. This combination of non-blamefulness and vulnerable self-disclosure is a fresh, genuine, and unexpected kind of confrontation that is much easier for your partner to deal with in a positive, caring, considerate way. Without the need to defend him- or herself and hearing clearly that you have been injured by his or her actions, your partner is free to initiate behavior that can help repair the damages rather than becoming defensive and resistant.

Hubby might say he's sorry and volunteer to clean up the mud. Wife can apologize for scolding and acknowledge how bad it must feel to get beaten up by both of you. The gambler can apologize, agree not to spend grocery money on lottery tickets again, and problem solve about paying the bills. The birthday-forgetter can apologize deeply, tell his wife how important she really is to him and empathize with her sadness (flowers and dinner out optional). The remote-toter can suggest some win-win problem solving around their television watching.

Too good to be true? Not really. Confrontation through self-disclosure often works immediately. But should the confrontation upset your mate, it is still likely to work eventually after you listen with empathy to the upset and then return to your self-disclosure so he or she can hear it again with less resistance.

Is this some kind of trick? A deceptive means of getting your own way by making your partner feel sorry for you? Not if you stick to the three conditions for growth: genuineness, acceptance, and empathy. It is very important that when you confront your partner you are congruent, honest, and genuine in your self-disclosure. If your partner is upset by being confronted—a predictable response, since no one likes getting confronted—empathize with his defensiveness. Then return to your congruent, genuine I-Message, knowing that when you both feel fully understood, the problem will be resolved or transformed.

CONFRONTATION CYCLE

Although non-blameful self-disclosure is likely to increase the possibility that your partner responds in a caring and cooperative way when you confront him or her about the behavior that is a problem for you, no one likes to be confronted. It always comes as some form of bad news, and it's likely to elicit some kind of defensive response from your partner. "I couldn't help it—the traffic was terrible." "Why are you always upset about this?" "You're taking it the wrong way."

The key to handling defensiveness—and ultimately, to clearing the pathway for your partner to respond caringly to your stated concern—is to shift gears immediately and power listen with real empathy to your partner's defensive response. "You had no idea the traffic would be so bad!" "You can't understand why this kind of thing bothers me so." "You think my response to this doesn't make much sense at all."

As in any instance when you work to hear and understand your partner's thoughts and feelings, power listening to him or her now helps your partner feel cared about and understood. This lowers his or her emotional temperature to the point that, after one or two rounds of heartfelt empathy from you, your partner is likely to be willing and able to hear your concern with open ears and an open heart. This gives you the chance to send your I-Message again, which may be somewhat modified now, after having released some of the emotion when you sent your original I-Message. As you shift back and forth from sending to listening, sending to listening, each of you eventually reaches the kind of emotional equilibrium that enables you to hear and understand each other fully. This kind of scenario opens the door to spontaneous behavior change on your partner's part, or it moves you both quite naturally into wanting to find a solution to this problem that will work for you both.

Thus, the **confrontation cycle** goes like this:

Non-blameful confrontation (through an I-Message) about your partner's behavior that is problemic for you.

Shifting gears to power listen to your partner's (likely) defensive response until his or her emotional temperature has cooled.
Resending your I-Message (likely a somewhat modified version).
Power listening to your partner's response (if necessary).

Continue through this cycle until either your partner volunteers helpful behavior change or you agree to problem solve together to find a mutually acceptable solution.

VULNERABILITY

The essence of genuine, congruent self-disclosure is **vulnerability**—the willingness to show your true thoughts and feelings and trust your partner to handle them caringly. It is about letting your partner know what is going on with you, where you are, what you think, what you feel, what you need.

Important caution: when you share your feelings as part of your I-Message, limit yourself to words that express emotion, like mad, sad, or glad. To help ensure this, never start a sentence with, "I feel that." Oddly enough, that phrase guarantees that you will utter an opinion or judgment instead of a feeling (e.g., "I feel that you did that on purpose to hurt me!"). "I feel that" immediately turns any confrontation into a critical You-Message and ends all pretense of vulnerability.

Paradoxically, making yourself vulnerable is one of the most powerful positions one can take. Animals in the wild lie down and show their bellies or their throats—their most vulnerable parts—to attacking members of their species, knowing that this will greatly reduce the likelihood that the other animal will kill them. When you fully reveal yourself in a confrontation, this vulnerability generates compassion for you and your needs.

Remember to reveal yourself when you confront, and remember when confronted, your partner will likely feel vulnerable, too. This will help you respond compassionately to him or her after the confrontation, and it will make it much easier for the two of you to find a way of handling the problem that will be acceptable to both of you.

YET AGAIN, THE IMPORTANCE OF ACCEPTANCE

Some of your spouse's annoying behaviors may best be handled by gaining a sense of perspective regarding your irritation. Ask yourself, is this behavior so out of line that I need to attend to it? Or am I just feeling cranky today? Can I find a way to feel more accepting in this case?

For myself (Ralph), Patty's tendency to be bossy or directive still pops up occasionally, even though she realizes it can be irritating. I still don't always like it when it appears, but I have come to see it as part of a larger characteristic I value and admire: her can-do drive to accomplish, to seize the day, to never take no for an answer. So now I greet it by reciting a mantra that brings me acceptance. I say to myself, "That's Patty!" and I smile. In many instances this gives me enough acceptance and emotional equilibrium that I don't have to confront.

Look for ways to become more accepting of some of your partner's idiosyncrasies. They are part of who your partner is. If you can accept them and honestly let them be, you will both be better off. Providing your partner with a climate of safety and genuine acceptance that fosters his or her growth as a human being is an important contribution you can make to the relationship. Everyone needs to receive acceptance from the person they love.

GUIDELINES FOR CONFRONTING YOUR PARTNER THROUGH AN I-MESSAGE

- Be clear and honest in describing the impact of your partner's behavior on you.
- Eliminate blame by mentally separating the culprit from the consequence, being clear that your partner is not "bad," but has simply chosen one way to meet a need that happens to interfere with one of your needs.
- Honor your partner's integrity—your partner has a right to get his or her needs met as well as to feel upset if he thinks your confrontation threatens them.

- Be prepared to shift gears to power listen with genuine empathy if your partner is defensive or upset at any point during the confrontation cycle.
- Have faith that your partner cares.

And, finally, keep in mind the importance of creating an accepting relationship with yourself. Everybody deserves compassion and acceptance, including you, and your capacity to be compassionate and accepting of others correlates to your ability to do that for yourself.

To recapitulate, we can't really change our partners because they are the product of their entire history, and they are entitled to be who they are. On the other hand, we can usually change behaviors that bother us by non-blamefully sharing the problem through vulnerable self-disclosure coupled with compassion and empathy. And the more accepting we can become of our wonderful mate, the fewer things we will want to change. These are important stepping stones on the path to a world class marriage.

（9）

PILLAR 9

KNOWING WHEN TO SURRENDER

There are defeats more triumphant than victories.

—Michel de Montaigne

In the course of your relationship, there will be a small number of your partner's behaviors, values, or characteristics that no amount of confronting or problem solving will resolve. These may be about matters large or small, but regardless of their importance, they can be the source of great pain between you.

Your partner may spend endless hours surfing the Internet, wear too much makeup for your taste, or spend too much money on an expensive hobby, and nothing in this book seems to bring helpful change from your partner or acceptance by you.

You then have three alternatives: continue to nag for change; become a silent but grumpy martyr; or surrender to the reality of who your partner really is. If you have been courageous and skillful in your attempts to achieve change and your loving partner has not been able to accommodate you, then the best alternative is the third one.

Paul came home from a trip to Sweden with a large viking ship chandelier he hoped to hang in the living room over the coffee table. When Kate saw it, she was shocked and couldn't imagine why Paul had bought it. She didn't want the large black iron sculpture anywhere in the house, much less hanging in the living room. Sincere attempts to resolve the conflict all ended in stalemate, with Paul still set on hanging his find in its place of prominence. A few days after the last attempt, Kate suddenly realized how deeply Paul's heart was set on displaying his trophy, and her objections melted away. She surrendered wholeheartedly, and now the chandelier has become an object of affection for both of them—for Kate because it represents an insight into something that mattered so much to her dear husband; for Paul, because of Kate's loving willingness to surrender to his great fondness for this unusual chandelier.

We describe another successful surrender in Pillar 10, when Patty surrendered to my strong need to feel well taken care of by cooking dinner for us each night at home. When she realized how symbolic this was for me, she surrendered her self-image as a seldom-cooking professional and gave me what I needed. She not only became a much better and more interested cook, but over the years I have come to enjoy cooking an occasional simple dinner myself and regularly handle the evening's kitchen cleanup. Her generous, unsacrificing surrender has brought us closer together in interesting ways.

The concept of **surrender** is for special, very infrequent cases where no other solution seems possible and where the one who surrenders can genuinely feel the compassion and empathy necessary for surrendering without sacrifice. However, the concept of surrender does not excuse permissiveness, passivity, or failure to take responsibility for meeting one's own needs with appropriate assertiveness.

Surrender means coming to terms with a deep need or fundamental characteristic of your partner that would be futile or very costly to change and transforming yourself so that you no longer wish your partner were different. You might do this through reading or research to expand your understanding and awareness; you might do it through meditation or prayer; you might do it by talking with a friend, family member, or counselor; you might do it through experimentation—"trying on" your partner's behavior to see if you can become more accepting of it that way; you might do it by simply making it your intention to surrender.

However it is that you surrender, it is magic. It releases you from tension and frustration, it releases your partner from disapproval and your attempts to change him or her, it bathes you both in understanding, acceptance, and closeness. Carefully chosen, surrender is a rare but important ingredient in a world class marriage.

FALSE ACCEPTANCE

A warning: beware of false acceptance—pretending your partner's behavior is okay with you in order to keep the peace or to look flexible while still seething about it inside. That is not surrender, and it can have dangerous repercussions. Besides the tension a phony surrender causes inside of you, it has a subtle distancing effect in the relationship caused by your need to disguise the disparity between your real self and the image you have created. Remember that honesty and congruence are essential components for relationship growth, both within yourself and with your partner, so for surrender to work, it must be genuine.

If the self-modification and surrender are real, based on new insights and understanding, there is an ironic outcome: differences in values, beliefs, or ways of doing things that at first seemed irreconcilable can be the source of poignant and very satisfying closeness—the pleasures of accepting the fact that your partner's behavior is a unique, funny, odd, quirky, distinctive aspect of a wonderful person who is different from you. (He likes viking chandeliers!)

You may be amazed to realize how truly accepting you can become of a quirk you previously had trouble accepting in your partner. Finding a way to accept your partner and a particular value or idiosyncrasy of his or hers can be a powerful affirmation that your partner has validity and integrity the way he or she is. It can be an important gift to the relationship. Everyone has the right to have certain idiosyncrasies left untrammeled and "unperfected" by their partner's efforts to change.

And surprisingly, after surrendering, you may even come to discover that there's nothing more endearing than seeing your partner continue in the behavior that once you wanted so much to change! This is a sweet joy of a world class marriage. And there is no more delicious gift than being accepted by your partner for who you are.

10

PILLAR 10

GIVING CARING
THE WAY IT MATTERS

Do unto your partner what your partner would have you do unto them.

—Harville Hendrix, relationship expert and
best-selling author of *Getting the Love You Want*

My (Patty's) father had a full-time job in addition to a home-based business. His workdays started at 8:00 a.m. and ended after I went to bed at night, and he worked on Saturdays. He never seemed to have time for me; he was always "too busy right now." He never wanted to talk about personal things or his feelings. He only told me that he loved me shortly before he died. I spent my childhood trying to get his approval, trying to avoid being in his way, and not feeling loved.

Did my father really love me? Absolutely. He loved me deeply, and he showed it the best way he knew how—by working hard to support the family and to make enough extra money so that my sister and I could attend good schools. Did this feel like love to me? Not at all! I felt that these acts were my birthright—any father should support his daughter and help her get a good education. That my father gave his all to do this for me didn't count for much. Only dimly did I feel loved by him, and I suffered for many years until therapy helped me understand and come to terms with my father's way of expressing love to his family. It is sad that my father's way of communicating this didn't really reach my heart until some years after he died.

Why? Gary Chapman's book *The Five Love Languages* identifies my father's love language as "acts of service," while mine happen to be "quality time" and "words of affirmation." My father showed his love in the way that had meaning for him, while I craved an entirely different emotional tongue. When this happens in your childhood, you endure feelings of sadness, deprivation, depression, self-doubt, pain, anger, bewilderment, and resentment.

If a similar mismatch of love languages happens in your marriage, as an adult you recognize that you have options. After enduring too much frustration about not feeling loved by your partner, one option open to you is divorce. Sadly, love language miscommunication is the source of many divorces that could otherwise have been prevented.

Although many couples don't automatically share mutual love languages, emotional estrangement and divorce aren't necessary if you each learn to show caring in a way that matters and in a language your beloved understands and values. To learn from your partner what this is, use I-Language and power listening to communicate and understand the love signals that are meaningful for each of you so that you can find the most satisfying ways of showing your love to each other.

Chapman identifies five **love languages**: words of affirmation, quality time, acts of service, receiving gifts, and physical touch. Words of affirmation is the classic love language that most people are familiar with, and it often forms an important part of the courtship ritual—statements such as "I love you"; "You look beautiful"; "You're so wonderful"; and "There's no one else like you" often accompany and define the sense of being in love and together as a couple. The other love languages— spending time doing enjoyable things together, doing thoughtful things to help your partner, giving unexpected loving gifts, and touching, caressing, and lovemaking are all ways that partners communicate their caring for each other. Each language is equally valid, but as each of us is unique, it's important—crucial—to learn from your partner what expressions of love, commitment, and caring carry the most weight in his or her world. There is no point in wasting your time giving, giving, giving, when it doesn't reach your partner's heart.

Like many women, I married a mini version of my father—Ralph's a borderline workaholic and it's easy for me to feel abandoned while he works hour after hour with loving care on the seemingly endless tasks associated with his job in addition to the conscientious handling of our finances and home maintenance. Do I feel loved by all these acts of service? Of course not! Although I appreciate the work he does, many times I feel abandoned, unhappy, and unloved whenever he spends too many extra hours doing these things—shades of my painful experience as a child and a common scenario in many marriages. Many nights I'd gladly trade after-dinner cleanup and morning coffee preparations for his immediate attention.

Fortunately, thanks to good communication, Ralph and I both recognize the danger in this combination of his long hours of work and my tendency to feel abandoned by it, so we officially set aside time every weekend to do something special together—"going on a toot," as we call it. Sometimes this is an elaborate plan to go someplace special; sometimes it's a walk on a nearby beach; sometimes it just means opening the sunroof of what we call our "toot car" while we go on an errand. Whatever it is that we do, we do it in recognition that this is something fun for us as a couple, something other than our daily activities, a time to experience our sense of closeness and love. With it, Ralph gives me the quality time I need to feel loved.

Obviously, one of Ralph's primary love languages is "acts of service." A few years into our relationship I was horrified to learn that what he most desired from me was to have a nice home-cooked dinner every night. I was horrified because cooking a wonderful dinner didn't fit with my self-image. ("I'm a professional, not a homemaker. It's beneath my dignity to put any effort into cooking!") His yearning for this was a terrible realization for me.

Yet from listening to him, I recognized the genuineness and deepness of this desire—his father and grandfather had owned a restaurant famous for its food, his mother had been a gourmet cook, and a good dinner just made him feel loved. After some soul-searching, I decided to surrender to Ralph (see chapter 9, "Knowing When to Surrender"). Determined to make nice dinners for him regularly, I somehow—rather magically, it seemed—became a better cook quickly, and Ralph became a much happier husband. One way to Ralph's heart is certainly through his stomach, and I couldn't feel good about myself as this worthwhile person's life partner if I didn't make an effort to express my love to him in one of the most important ways he can experience it, with this act of service.

Dating couples whose ways of communicating caring are markedly different often drift apart quickly. They experience themselves as being "too different" from each other and the relationship flounders. Others don't discover their differences until after marriage or after they move in together.

> Brad and Judy moved in together after knowing each other for two years while they were both in graduate school. Their relationship was strong and the move symbolized their commitment. Shortly after setting up their joint household, Judy's behavior changed. Rather than being the loving and attentive person Brad had known at school, she started putting a great deal of energy into housekeeping. Brad felt like he was living with another person, and he really missed the loving and attentive partner he was used to. Brad shared his frustration and sadness about this with Judy and learned—somewhat to his amazement—that she had been trying to show her love for him by making a lovely home like her mother had kept for her father. After learning that he didn't care much about how clean the house was or if his shirts were ironed, Judy agreed to minimize these activities and spend more time having fun and being affectionate with Brad.

Learning to show your caring in ways that matter to your partner is essential. For many of us, this results in stretching ourselves to become comfortable communicating in ways that seem foreign. Making dinner was certainly not my preferred way of showing Ralph my feelings of love, and my first reaction was to resist the whole idea.

MARRIAGE AND GROWTH

To avoid getting stuck in such resistance, it's helpful to remember that marriage is life's primary spawning ground for growth. Marriage is the arena in which we deal with another human being in thousands of situations over a period of many years. The depth and breadth of this experience provide endless challenges. We cannot expect that "who we are" when we first become a couple is a complete enough person to respond in a satisfying way to all the needs that will arise over the years of the relationship. "Who we are" needs to change—we need to grow, expand, learn new skills, communicate in new ways, increase our understanding and acceptance of others, expand our intellectual and emotional repertoires, and learn how to give our partner caring that really counts to him or her.

Being in a committed relationship provides one of life's biggest opportunities to become more fully developed as a person. If we don't respond to those challenges, we cheat our partner and we cheat ourselves out of the opportunity of knowing the fullness, richness, and beauty that lies within us. Had I stuck to my position that, as a professional, I shouldn't be expected to cook a good dinner, I'd have missed the chance to show my caring for Ralph in a way that really counts for him. I'd also have missed the chance to expand my skills as a human being, as well as to expand my self-image, moving beyond a narrow view of myself as a "professional" into a new self-definition that encompasses more complexity—that of a professional who also cooks. My willingness to show caring in this way that mattered to Ralph resulted in benefits for us both.

Of course, when you attempt new things, they feel strange. Unless you're a native speaker of French, your first efforts to speak the language feel awkward, even bizarre. It doesn't seem like you. You don't feel comfortable with the language, and you are afraid of ridicule for speaking it badly. Any new behavior is that way. When you learn from your partner more about the ways she or he would like you to express your love, you will likely feel that you're being asked to speak a foreign language. It won't feel natural, and you need to expect that and find a way to tolerate this strangeness.

"Why am I vacuuming the house to show her my love when I'd much rather be giving her a nice massage?"

"Why do I have to keep telling her I love her? I thought fixing her car said pretty much the same thing!"

"Why do we have to go to the ball game? I would just like to sit on the couch together and talk."

"Why does she want flowers? I tell her I love her every day!"

Why? Because if you express caring in ways that matter to your partner, she or he will get maximum value from it, and you'll get maximum impact for your efforts. The efficiency of this shouldn't be ignored. We call it "cost-effective caring." And your beloved deserves to experience at least some of your love and caring in a language that resonates the most.

Remember, life is never static, and marriage is about growth. Learn to speak new languages, learn to find multiple ways to express yourself, grow yourself, and you will grow your partner's sense of happiness with your love.

PILLAR 11

HANDLING HOT TOPICS

Life is sexually transmitted.

—Anonymous

Sex and money are like any other subjects that couples have to deal with—except the emotional stakes are higher. People's feelings run stronger and are accompanied by irrationality, vulnerability, and greater concern about the outcome. That's why these subjects are hot. It's important to gird yourself with sensitivity and communication skills so that these important topics are resolved with the highest possible satisfaction for both partners. Otherwise, feelings are badly hurt and your relationship suffers greatly.

The key to success in dealing with sex, money, in-laws, or any emotionally loaded topic is world class communication—listening with sensitivity and empathy, expressing your needs and preferences with vulnerable self-disclosure, and handling conflicts and disagreements in ways that work for both partners.

INSIGHTS TO MAKE YOUR SEX LIFE SIZZLE

One basic thing you need to know about sex is: when you're hot, you're hot, when you're not, you're not. (And the same goes for your partner.)

Recognize this; this is reality. And when one of you is lukewarm, it means that the door *may* be open. Talk with your partner about what she or he might like. Using sweet talk, gentle rubbing, dancing, or massage, things might heat up!

If you're not getting what you want, ask for it by name. Don't expect your partner to read your mind or fulfill some dream you've never mentioned. Remember, relationship satisfaction is all about meeting needs. Taking responsibility for communicating them is the first step. Give your partner the opportunity to please you by sharing with him or her what matters to you sexually.

Don't leave it all to chance. Make time for love, the same way you make time for sports or seeing friends. Legitimize sex as one of the most significant, important, necessary, and enjoyable activities in your lives. As the saying goes, "All work and no play makes Jack a dull boy."

Use the magic of "No." If you're hot, but she or he's not, try this: ask for a strong yes or no answer to the question, "Do you want to make love right now?" If the answer is yes, you're all set. If the answer is no, then increase the strength of the no answer by probing, "Are you sure?" If your partner answers, "Yes, I'm sure!" respond nicely with, "Okay." Then wait a few moments and ask again. Surprisingly, when your partner can say "no" and still feel accepted by you, the feeling frequently passes, leaving the door open for feelings of love to rush in. This is welcome and convincing proof of the adage that all feelings are transitory if they can be fully expressed and accepted. Try it, you'll like it!

SEX AS NONVERBAL COMMUNICATION

Sex is the ultimate form of nonverbal communication. Its powerful body language can range from a sidelong glance, a soft caress, a gentle kiss, a sigh, to all-entangling, gasping sexual union.

As clear and satisfying as it often is, nonverbal communication can also be ambiguous, occasionally causing couples to misread each other's nonverbal cues—making assumptions about each other's preferences and feelings that are totally erroneous. For example, in the early, tentative stages of testing for mutual interest in making love, one partner might interpret a random movement as a rebuff when no rebuff was intended; pulling away might be an adjustment to accommodate a shoulder ache, not a rejection to the partner's advances. To guard against such hurtful and discouraging misinterpretations, it's important to summon the courage to communicate verbally about unclear nonverbal cues, to check the accuracy of your understanding and to avoid mistaken assumptions that can curtail sexual pleasure.

Because our emotions are so closely tied up with our sexuality and our desire to be pleasing to and satisfied by our partner is so great, communication about sex is a vulnerable arena. To ensure that you are sensitive and gentle enough in talking about your sexual needs and assumptions, remember to use self-disclosing I-Language for your communication and power listening when your partner talks about his or her needs. This approach will help you to share deeply and intimately, and it will greatly increase your ability to meet your own and your partner's fondest sexual desires. In addition, as your communication skills grow and the 16 Pillars of a world class marriage infuse the other areas of your lives, your lovemaking will be a principal beneficiary of your heightened relationship, and your hot will be hotter.

SEX AS A WAY TO GROW

Sex is the ultimate balancing act between selflessness and selfishness. In order for it to be mutually satisfying for you and your partner, you must achieve this balance and find a satisfying sexual language that the two of you share. When we are young and our hormones are raging, this balance comes more easily. It may not seem like a balancing act at all—you're both eager, and everything is exciting and satisfying. You start to see the issues a few years into a marriage and after hormone levels decline.

To achieve sexual satisfaction, you need to know what you want, you need to have the courage to communicate it to your partner, and you need to have the sense of self it takes to go for it. All of this requires strength and confidence, and for many of us, it takes personal growth.

For your partner to achieve satisfaction sexually with you, it takes strength and confidence on his or her part, and it takes sensitivity and selflessness on yours. You may also need to stretch yourself beyond the limits of what comes naturally to you so that you can be a satisfying partner. It's easy to disparage your partner's sexual preferences as stupid, inappropriate, unnecessary, vulgar, awkward, boring, or embarrassing. But remember, criticism and blame aren't helpful, and your partner has a right to get his or her sexual needs met—just as everyone does. Sex, like all issues you deal with together, is about finding mutually agreeable solutions. To the extent that you can grow and genuinely expand your capacity for flexibility in regard to your partner's favorite sexual solutions, you will make it easier for your partner to get his or her needs met.

Thus, sexual satisfaction, like all aspects of a marriage relationship, is ultimately about growth—about growing fuller understandings of your own needs and how to communicate about them and get them met with your partner; about growing greater compassion and flexibility in helping your partner get his or her needs met; about defining personal ways of experiencing together the special physical pleasures of yourselves as a couple.

Sex is sex, but it's a lot more, too. Like many other aspects of marriage, sex gives you a golden opportunity to grow as a human being and expand the level of satisfaction you get from your relationship. David Schnarch's book *Passionate Marriage* is an excellent resource for helping you define yourself sexually and for realizing your sexual potential in your relationship with your partner. If you choose to hide sexual frustrations from yourself and your partner, you lose the benefits of personal growth, physical satisfaction, and deep intimacy with your beloved.

KEYS THAT UNLOCK THE DOOR
TO MUTUAL MONEY MANAGEMENT

Money is another hot topic in marriage, and the source of much wrangling between couples. Yet, like all hot topics, when you find successful ways to talk and problem solve together about money issues, it can become a source of closeness and connection between the two of you. Besides the importance of using good communication skills whenever you talk about money, there are other keys to success.

Become aware of how large a role fear and anxiety play in you and your partner's attitudes and behaviors regarding money and develop genuine compassion for both of your shortcomings in dealing with it.

We tend to think that managing money—a seemingly logical, mathematical, cut-and-dried process—ought to be dealt with rationally. We often tell ourselves that we do. But irrationality can easily take the upper hand with money. Without knowing it, one partner is hit by fears that she or he is inadequate to manage it effectively, that she or he will lose it all, or that she or he won't have enough to pay the bills. Another might overspend out of denial, to kill the anxiety, or to prove there's enough. Many people have strong, irrational desires to have possessions that validate their worth. To our partner, struggling with his or her own financial demons, we may appear to be tightwads, spendthrifts, selfish, controlling, foolish, impossible, or nuts.

As long as the highly emotional nature of money management is hidden under the cloak of rationality, successful money management is hard to come by. In this area of your relationship, you need to exercise great compassion and nurture the skills of empathy, acceptance, and genuineness, which will allow you both to grow stronger in this area.

Within the context of the potential craziness surrounding money, it is valuable to recognize that, deep down, your partner would like nothing better than to meet all your needs and give you everything you've ever wanted. Your partner is likely to feel sad and frustrated if she or he can't. And you'd like to do the same, and you feel the same frustration. Therefore, buried underneath all the rational arguments, there is the wonderful good news that each of you wants to meet every one of your partner's needs. Do yourselves a favor by expressing these generous desires and feelings, bringing them into the open, where they can nurture your understanding of how to manage your money together. You won't have the money to buy it all, but it nurtures the relationship to know that your partner wants the world for you.

> Marsha always loved jewelry and wished Alex would give her jewelry for her birthday, but her husband thought it was a waste of money. Moreover, their finances were tight, and there really wasn't much money to spend on non-necessities. In talking about this, Alex revealed that he felt trapped in a double bind: to buy Marsha jewelry felt like a bad use of their limited

resources; not to buy jewelry ran the risk of greatly disappointing his wife. Through power listening, Marsha gained understanding and compassion for Alex's dilemma. Hearing that his wife understood this released a lot of tension for Alex. He realized that despite his personal feelings about jewelry, he wanted Marsha to be happy, and that if jewelry made her happy, then he wanted her to have it. This mutual understanding and caring about each other's needs felt good to them both. Even though no jewelry was actually purchased for this birthday, their deep sharing diminished this subject as a source of difficulty and irritation for them both.

To the extent that you can, set up your organizational system for handling money with your partner so that you have a sense of being "in it" together. It's okay to have some separate funds. However, don't overlook the opportunities for emotional closeness that can result from having money as a mutual cornerstone of your partnership. ("We've saved enough for a down payment!" "We've got enough for a vacation!") Sharing money and sharing decisions about its use give you the opportunity to nurture your feelings of being close, of being together. Money can be a catalyst for great communication and closeness. Use it as a way to deepen the relationship.

Ralph inherited some money from his parents several years ago and invested it with moderate success, yet he always felt concerned that he wasn't managing the money well. After listening to his grumbling about this and mulling over his suggestion that I take over the job of managing his inheritance, I took on the task. This opened up a whole new area of study for me that has been fascinating. Since California law dictates that inherited money is not community property, Ralph's inheritance is not legally mine at all; nevertheless, this is a wonderful source of sharing for us.

HEART-TO-HEART CONNECTION

A closing thought about the volatile areas of sex and money: at all times, remember the importance of keeping the **heart-to-heart connection** between you and your partner. This is the invisible thread between the two of you that affirms, "No matter what else happens, our love, our relationship, our caring is what is constant; it is what matters." Staying conscious of this and holding it inviolate helps you communicate in a caring, sharing way and protects the relationship while you are resolving these difficult issues. Sometimes when Ralph and I have been having a difficult discussion, he puts his hand up to his chest and then moves it from his heart toward mine. This immediately melts my heart and calms our conversation.

(12)

PILLAR 12

RESOLVING CONFLICTS
AND DISAGREEMENT

Agreement is made more precious by disagreement.

—Publilius Syrus

When two people share their lives in an intensive and long-term way, they have disagreements. The subject matter ranges from the trivial (which movie to see tonight) to the serious (how to handle a rebellious child). Most of these are easily resolved through good will and clear communication, but others prove more stubborn, sometimes escalating into serious arguments and fights, with emotions running high. Here are some things to think about in regard to the stubborn ones.

Having occasional heated words is normal. It may even be exhilarating. It may clear the air. If its jolt of high energy is accompanied by a reasonable resolution, the relief may even lead to sex. However, heated fights or drawn-out arguments are not welcome if (A) one partner always dominates and wins; (B) they occur with predictable frequency and regularity; (C) they are never satisfactorily resolved; or—it goes without saying—(D) they are accompanied by physical violence. This chapter explores the dynamics of disagreement and resolution with the goal of enabling you to embrace and manage this basic aspect of a close relationship with confidence and success.

HELPFUL PILLARS

The secret of managing most conflicts and disagreements—to prevent, defuse, or quickly resolve them—is the conscious use of the knowledge and tools you already learned in the previous chapters. These include avoiding blame (chapter 2), avoiding tit for tat (chapter 5), avoiding flippancy, irony, and other "cool" talk (chapter 7), recognizing and handling the hidden fears that make some subjects unusually volatile (chapter 11), and most especially, the communication tools of power listening and vulnerable self-disclosure described in chapters 4 and 8. In their own ways, these all emphasize empathy, genuineness, and acceptance—qualities fundamental to resolving differences as well as in promoting growth. As you progress in your understanding of and ability to use these gentle but powerful ideas and tools, fewer disagreements will reach conflict status.

Let's look at how these notions might apply. Suppose Janet is using the computer to research a project in the evening when Ted wants to go online to read and answer his e-mail.

They could blame each other:

"You're always on the damned computer when I want to use it!" "If your e-mail is that important, why didn't you have the sense to answer it when you first got home?"

Or he could tit for tat:

"You used it last night. Now it's my turn!"

Or she could express her anger with sarcastic cool talk:

"You think your e-mail is *that* important? Gimme a break!"

It is easy to see how these common approaches raise the stakes of a minor difficulty. In contrast, Ted and Janet will find it much easier to work things out by turning to self-disclosure and empathy.

Janet:

"I hear that you'd like to use the computer now, but my deadline for this project is so close that I'm scared stiff I'm not going to make it if I don't finish this research tonight."

Ted:

"Gee, I didn't realize you were so under the gun. I'll finish up the book I'm reading while you work and answer my email before we go to bed."

Avoiding needless provocation and using good communication to understand and accept each other's needs and feelings resolves the great majority of ordinary disagreements.

CONFLICT MANAGEMENT

Occasionally, however, no quick accommodation is apparent, and each partner's interests feel so important to them personally that the obvious options seem unworkable. These are the difficult situations. Here are some examples:

Sally is eager to landscape the backyard, putting in a shaded patio, pathways, and gardens. Jason likes the backyard the way it is and is upset by the prospect of spending the money that remodeling would require.

Peg wants their son to enjoy the experience of going away to summer camp, but Dan feels strongly that it would be better for the boy to attend the summer swim program at the neighborhood YMCA and continue carrying his paper route.

Gary has a passion for fishing on Saturday mornings. Pat wants very much for them to do something together as a couple on Saturdays but hates fishing.

When the disagreements are strong and feelings run high, it is essential to a world class relationship that both partners share a commitment to finding solutions that meet the needs of both parties and that they have a workable method for reaching that goal, as well as handling the anger and upset that typically accompany conflict.

Without such a method for conflict resolution, one party's interests are accommodated while the other party's are frustrated, regardless of who wins or who loses. Either way, the loser feels resentful and the winner feels guilty, and this inevitably damages the good feelings the partners have for each other. It doesn't matter who is resentful. Resentment always causes relationship damage, and neither of you can afford that.

If, however, the conflict is resolved by moving beyond an argument into a process for discovering creative, expanded options that meet both partners' real needs, many benefits ensue. First, both partners feel satisfied and cared about, rather than resentful or guilty. Second, both partners are accepting of the solution and both cooperate willingly. Third, after having turned a potentially bruising situation into a shared victory, the partners have a sense of achievement, successful teamwork, and an increased sense of closeness. And finally, such a process can produce surprising creativity that has exciting applications to other aspects of their lives.

Many years ago, Ralph and I had a conflict about taking a vacation. Our initial positions were that I wanted to take one, Ralph didn't. Digging beneath those opposing postures, we found that I needed a change of pace and some fun. And Ralph felt the same but also felt a strong need not to spend the money he expected a vacation would cost. Once we identified those needs, we set out to find a solution that would meet my needs for change and fun but wouldn't conflict with Ralph's need not to spend too much money.

The solution we decided upon was to take a vacation in our own home. We packed our suitcases and departed from our bedroom on Friday at 6:00 p.m. and "moved" into the guestroom for a week. We ate breakfast at home each day on different plates than we usually used, sitting around the coffee table in the living room rather than at the dining table. No housework or yard work was allowed after 10 a.m., after which we set out as tourists in our hometown, enjoying a different local attraction each day. Never during the week did we open the door to our bedroom, enjoying instead the newness of being together in the guestroom. And with no airfare or hotel rooms to pay for, it was a marvelous low-cost vacation that still brings us fond memories.

Our ability to find a solution to this problem was exhilarating. Instead of breeding frustration and resentment, this solution to our conflict brought us joy, increased closeness, and became one of our fondest memories together.

NEGOTIATING METHODS

We reached that agreement by following a very clear method of conflict resolution developed by Dr. Thomas Gordon in *P.E.T.: Parenting Effectiveness Training* and *L.E.T.: Leader Effectiveness Training* books and programs (see bibliography). His method is based on the work of American educator John Dewey's pragmatic, six-step formula for solving any problem. Dewey's steps were: (1) defining the problem; (2) generating all possible solutions; (3) evaluating solutions generated; (4) selecting the most promising; (5) implementing the solution; and (6) following up to see if the solution worked. Gordon modified the formula to work specifically with conflicts by recasting step one as "defining the problem in terms of both parties' needs," and step two as "generating solutions that will meet both of those sets of needs."

Together with communication skills for handling each party's upset feelings, this reformulation produced a powerful and effective way to handle conflicts, which we used to our advantage when the vacation issue arose.

Another useful set of conflict management tools was created by Roger Fisher and William Ury in their book, *Getting to Yes* (see bibliography). The authors identify two major barriers to successful negotiation: the participants see their original positions as the only solutions, and the participants believe that the only bargaining chip available is giving up fractional pieces of those positions.

For example, a vendor says, "The price is $50." The tourist says, "I'll give you ten." (These are their positions.) The vendor then inches down, and the tourist inches up, and maybe they'll meet in the middle and strike a bargain, or maybe they won't. In this scenario, no option other than compromise—where each party loses something—is possible.

If we had stuck with our positions, I (Ralph) might have inched up (slowly) about how much money I'd be willing to spend, while Patty inched down (slowly) on her expectations—how desirable a vacation destination and how long we could be away. Maybe we'd have gone on a vacation, maybe not, but neither of us would have been really satisfied. But by giving up your initial positions and focusing on the real interests, you experience an entirely different climate for the negotiation or conflict-resolution process, and the door opens to elegant and unexpected solutions.

Fisher and Ury teach how to move beyond initial positions, and they also write in detail about how to deal effectively with the other's emotions and misperceptions (as well as your own), how to discover the true interests and needs behind the positions, how to increase the range of options, and—of course—how to get to yes.

All three books—*P.E.T.: Parenting Effectiveness Training*, *L.E.T.: Leader Effectiveness Training*, and *Getting to Yes*—give clear, detailed methods not only for resolving difficult issues, but also for using them as creative opportunities to deepen and strengthen relationships through the joy and excitement of solving challenging problems together. We urge you to jump-start your own conflict-management skills by utilizing these or any other resources that help you develop your capacity to find solutions that work for both of you. Having confidence that the two of you know how and are both committed to finding mutually acceptable solutions whenever you have a conflict will go a long way toward helping you both feel safe and cared for in the relationship.

COUPLES WITHOUT CONFLICTS

Some couples say that they never fight. While that sounds wonderful, it may be a danger sign, as couples who never have disagreements are more likely to divorce than couples who do. The reason? Disagreements between people in a close relationship are inevitable, and if a couple reports none, the strong likelihood is that one or both parties is giving in at the slightest hint of disagreement in order to keep the peace. This usually means that an unending series of unmet needs—whether large or small—has been growing inside one or both partners, with secret resentment over those losses building beneath feigned contentment. This resentment eventually forms a bitter though silent barrier between the two of them, and over time, closeness and caring break down. Then discouragement sets in, and the stage is set for divorce. Consider Madelyn:

> Madelyn never challenged Edward about anything. Edward worked late many nights, and she never complained. She let him select where

they lived, their cars, their friends, where they went for vacations. She acquiesced in every disagreement, large or small. She did everything she thought a good wife should do. Their friends remarked that they seemed the perfect couple—never a cross word. One day, without warning, Madelyn packed her clothes, moved out, and soon filed for divorce. She wrote a note saying that she had "had enough" and never spoke to Edward again.

If you "never have a cross word," you may need to reexamine your conflict-management practices to ensure that no one is tossing resentments into a gunny sack that will eventually be stuffed so full that it erupts like Mt. Vesuvius.

RECOGNIZING AND HELPING A SACRIFICER

Some people are simply fight-phobic. They are highly susceptible to using a permissive, need-sacrificing conflict-resolution style, as Madelyn did. Besides eroding the relationships with pent-up resentment, such people have difficulty getting their needs met in any conflict. Most of us would prefer not to fight, especially with our partner, but some people are profoundly unwilling or unable to tolerate conflict.

If this is you, chances are that your fight phobia stems from a pattern of being consistently overpowered in earlier conflicts, either as a child by your parents or other adults, or more recently in your relationship with your spouse. It's valuable to identify whether your conflict avoidance comes from previous bad experiences in childhood or from your present relationship. If you recognize that the problem stems from your childhood, it is important for you to be consciously aware and realize that your fear of sticking up for your needs in a conflict with your spouse is due to past fears, not present dangers. This will help you relate to your partner more realistically. If that is the case, acknowledge to your partner your awareness of this problem and ask her or him to assist in any way possible to help you communicate your needs whenever conflict occurs. With such support and by learning a dependable process (such as Gordon's or Fisher and Ury's methods) for resolving differences, you can eventually become more assertive regarding your needs.

If you have had previous bad experiences with a partner who has been unwilling to work with you to find mutually acceptable solutions to conflicts and who insists on getting his or her way, then it is important that you find the courage to confront your partner and communicate your needs and feelings in this area. You need to say something like this:

> "I realize that there have been times in the past when you have imposed your decisions on me and I let you do that. But I am unwilling to let this happen any more. I want us to handle our conflicts differently from now on so that you and I both get our needs met. Are you willing to make this change with me?"

If you have an essentially loving relationship, it's likely that your partner will eventually be open to this change, although you need to realize that if your partner has been winning every disagreement, a demand for such a change will not be welcomed. So you can expect to hear such defensive responses as, "I've never been unfair to you about anything." Try to listen to this empathically to help your partner handle those defensive feelings (e.g., "You're shocked that I see myself losing to you a lot.")

After you are sure that you have understood your partner's feelings, communicate your message again, after which you may need to listen again, and so on, until your partner feels comfortable enough to problem solve this important issue. Gradually, you and your partner will come to a shared understanding about mutually acceptable solutions to your conflicts. Then work on developing good conflict-resolution skills so that you can handle future conflicts successfully together.

If—after confronting cleanly and doing your best to handle your partner's defensive reactions—she or he still refuses to commit to a mutually acceptable process for resolving future conflicts, you may be faced with a difficult reality. A spouse who is unwilling to acknowledge that your needs are as important as his or her own needs is not really offering you much. If there is willingness to change, a therapist or marriage counselor might be able to help your partner deal with whatever difficulties underlie the inability to respect your right to get your needs met. Should your partner be unwilling to commit to such a process of personal change, you may need to reevaluate the relationship. This would be a difficult issue to face, but all human beings deserve to get their needs met—including you.

THE IMPORTANCE OF CONFLICT

How you and your partner resolve conflict is a strong predictor of the level of satisfaction in your relationship. Good times are wonderful, and it's important to invest in them and build your positive connections together. But conflicts occur. Consistently ignoring them or giving in to keep the peace can undermine much of what is otherwise good between you. On the other hand, because conflicts are so emotionally powerful, the experience of working together to find satisfying solutions, especially when achieving success seems impossible, stimulates powerful feelings of pride, closeness, and trust.

So learn to embrace conflicts and disagreements as the opportunities they surely are. World class marriages are singularly enhanced by courageous and caring conflict resolution and sensitive handling of disputes. Commit together to finding solutions and developing the communication and negotiating skills necessary to ensure your mutual success when conflicts occur. With commitment and skills, conflict can be transformed into important building blocks of your relationship.

13

PILLAR 13

GIVING APOLOGY AND FORGIVENESS

A friend recently told us about a twenty-fifth-anniversary party where the husband gave a toast and said, "The key to our success is very simple. Within minutes after every fight, one of us says, 'I'm sorry, Sally.'"

—Cokie and Steve Roberts

APOLOGY

Apologies are magic. They have the power to erase the problem and to bring about forgiveness and closeness. No matter how hard you try to please your partner and meet your partner's needs, it's inevitable that you will at some time say or do something that hurts your partner. Even when feelings are hurt, it is never too late to go back and clean it up, and you can do this by acknowledging to your partner that you know that your behavior was hurtful and that you sincerely regret causing that pain. You cannot just say the words; you must feel remorse and communicate this fully. Really let your partner see that you regret your action. Be genuine.

Difficult as it may be, it is important to acknowledge that you were wrong or did something wrong. Denying your culpability can make your partner feel frustrated or even crazy. Avoid contaminating your apology with a justification for why you did what you did—this is the time to admit your mistake and express regret, not an opportunity to mitigate blame. Nothing increases the success of an apology more than a heartfelt, "I was wrong," as hard as it may be to admit. When you apologize truthfully from the heart, your partner is likely to be willing to forgive you. If your partner cannot forgive you right away, allow him or her the opportunity to work through his or her continuing anger or pain. Sometimes it takes time for these feelings to subside, even if you have apologized genuinely. At those times, open yourself to listening with empathy.

Remember that all feelings are transient, even these. Feelings come, and they go. When you listen to, accept, and acknowledge your partner's rebuff of your mea culpa, his or her hurt feelings may lose their emotional grip and subside. When they do, a full, heartfelt apology will probably be accepted.

The key steps in apologizing are accessed through the three conditions that promote growth—empathy, acceptance, and genuineness:

1. Empathize with your partner so that you can understand his or her hurt, which opens the door to your admission to yourself that your behavior has hurt your partner.
2. Accept responsibility for doing something that has hurt your partner, which enables you to acknowledge to yourself that you were wrong, mistaken, or acted badly in some way.
3. Genuinely acknowledge this to your partner and express genuine regret.
4. Listen to and acknowledge any additional pain your partner expresses.
5. Repeat that you are sorry to have done something so hurtful to your partner and acknowledge fully any culpability you may bear.
6. Remember that your partner may or may not be able to forgive you right away.
7. Remember that you are a worthwhile person, even if your partner is unable to forgive you.

Some people grow up in families where the parents never apologize to the children for anything they have done. In families where apologizing is not modeled, it is hard for the child to learn how to apologize. Instead, the child learns to defend his or her behavior—to cover it up, to justify it, to pretend that the behavior wasn't so bad. When these children grow to be adults, it can be very hard for them to apologize. If this is your partner, cut him or her as much slack as possible when it's his or her turn to apologize. If you are like me (Patty), it helps to remember that everyone is fallible. To have made a mistake or to have hurt your partner does not make you an unworthy human being. Work on your self-acceptance and on developing the strength to acknowledge your mistakes. This is an important ingredient in creating a world class marriage.

FORGIVENESS

Forgiveness is apology's alter ego. Every marriage must deal with hurtful words or actions, however large or small. After they occur, both partners need to engage in relationship repair. The transgressor must acknowledge his or her offensive behavior and apologize for it, but after receiving the apology, the person who has been hurt must move toward forgiveness.

Alexander Pope said, "to forgive is divine." Through the "divinity" of forgiveness, the relationship experiences a reviving balm that rekindles feelings of closeness. In some circumstances, the lack of forgiveness can itself cause the relationship to suffer severely. When one partner refuses to forgive the other, for whatever reason, the breach caused by the transgression remains unhealed, damaging the relationship.

Unwillingness to forgive can come from different sources. Sometimes a partner refuses to forgive the other as a way to maintain the upper hand or some kind of control or to punish the other for the hurtful words or deeds. Or forgiveness may be withheld because the hurt feels too large to forgive. But it is important to recognize that, whatever the reason, if the offending partner is not forgiven after a full and sincere apology, then the hurt party is causing the relationship to remain in limbo. There may be times and circumstances when this is appropriate, but usually it is not. In a loving relationship, most hurts are not worth threatening the relationship. Therefore, it is important to develop the capacity to forgive, so that the damage heals and the relationship can continue.

Pouting

Perhaps the most common barrier to forgiving your partner is the attractiveness of staying angry as a way to punish him or her for how bad you feel or to make sure she or he will never do it again. **Pouting** or sulking is used often because it—perversely—feels so good. "I'll show him how bad he hurt me!" we say to ourselves. But—attractive as it may seem—pouting is a destructive way to manipulate your partner and should be recognized as such. And it tends to reap its just reward. As a former devoted sulker, I (Ralph) enjoyed acting very polite but distant (my well-polished technique), but after several days of my continued cold shoulder, Patty's welcome contrition turned to anger. Then the window of opportunity for recovering closeness banged shut, until I was finally forced to apologize for pouting.

When it is difficult to accept your partner's apology, it helps to put the transgression into perspective. Try to examine it objectively. In marital relationships, probably the most frequent causes of hurt are words— words of blame, criticism, anger. Many times your partner's words are not intended to hurt and are said only to avoid feeling out of control in a situation or to prevail in an argument, and they are blurted out without thinking. After responding to your partner's apology by authentically expressing your remaining hurt, use your listening skills to hear his or her plea for forgiveness and strive to empathize deeply enough to understand the human need behind your partner's hurtful words. This compassion may soften your hurt and help you forgive.

CONNECTIONS TO THE PAST

Another possible source of empathy as an aid to forgiveness lies in recognizing situations where your partner's anger or criticism seems out of proportion to the circumstances and not compatible with the deep feelings you know she or he has for you. At those times, the heated words may stem from a similarity between the present situation with you and a painful one from your partner's past. At these times, the deepest emotional component of your partner's flare-up has very little to do with you and your relationship; the situation merely resembles an earlier one locked in the recesses of your partner's mind. Your partner's emotional outburst carries with it leftover emotion from the earlier situation—often a childhood experience involving a parent or authority figure. This is sometimes called "an earlier similar," and these are often responsible for emotional "plug-ins," which cause undue emotional intensity to erupt over a current situation.

A by-product of a marital relationship is that the emotional bond between partners is so deep that it connects us unconsciously with parental figures from our past, with whom many of us have unresolved emotional hurts. It is important to recognize this likelihood in your relationship together, as it will help you see why you or your partner may say or do things that otherwise seem inappropriate to the current reality of your generally loving relationship.

When you recognize an out-of-proportion reaction, the path to forgiveness may be to discuss the possibility with your partner. Tell him or her that the outburst seemed out of character, that you're having a hard time accepting his or her apology, that you suspect the outburst was caused by a deep emotional echo from the past, and ask if he or she is willing to examine that possibility. Then use empathic power listening to his or her response. You may learn how this situation with you somehow plugged into painful emotions from the past, which can help you develop compassion and forgiveness for the transgression. You may also learn a lot about the tender, vulnerable parts of your partner and develop greater intimacy.

Remember, when your partner's behavior is louder, stronger, or more hurtful than seems warranted, it may be a sign of some emotional loading from the past that has attached itself to the present situation. This knowledge can prevent you from escalating the situation and help you dredge up the capacity to offer the healing balm of compassion and if needed, forgiveness.

But what if you are the one who is plugged into the past? Perhaps your partner's words or deeds were not actually as unforgivable as they seemed but only appeared to be because they were similar to painful criticism or angry outbursts reminiscent of your childhood, when you were more vulnerable and dependent than you are as an adult. A continued inability to forgive after receiving a heartfelt apology may be a guidepost pointing toward a search for past pain that could result in being able to put your partner's transgression in perspective and find the way to forgive.

THE ROLE OF THERAPY

Everyone experiences problems during their childhood—whether from specific experiences with their parents, teachers, friends, or just the general adversities of life—and most people have some scars from those experiences. The main job of childhood is to learn a very complex set of skills needed for survival. Often, a common and unfortunate by-product of this extended learning process is that we come to feel inadequate or unloved. In an earnest attempt to help us, parents, teachers, or others inadvertently say or do things that hurt us during our childhood. Even more insidious is the fact that our childhood experiences are processed through a child's brain, which is not yet fully developed. As a result, each of us inevitably misinterprets many situations because our young brain just wasn't capable of subtle perceptions or interpretations. As a result, we come out of these early experiences feeling vaguely (and perhaps very strongly) stupid, crazy, unwanted, unacceptable, unloved, unlovable.

In many cases, a more refined brain would have made very different inferences. However, for all of us, the reality is that when we were four years old, we had the brain of a four year old, which limited our ability to make appropriate inferences from sometimes complex situations. Added to this is the fact that our personal interpretations of our childhood experiences make very strong grooves in our psyche, and somehow these interpretations become ingrained as "reality." These experiences can be scarring; they can badly damage our self-esteem and can be extremely painful. Furthermore, they can make it hard—sometimes impossible—for us to experience satisfaction in our adult relationships.

One of the jobs of adulthood is to deal with those scars—to process the hurts, reinterpret past situations, forgive others, forgive yourself, learn from mistakes, and somehow to let go of the past and live in the present. As an ongoing process, most of us carry some unresolved problems from the past that cause enhanced pain in the present, and it's always a worthwhile investment to work on resolving these sources of pain. Much of this work can be done on your own—especially if you have insight into your problems or a facilitative friend or partner. This is traditionally the work of therapy, although therapy is not available to everyone and is generally expensive. If it is an option for you, it may be a worthwhile investment to enhance your personal freedom and the well-being of your marriage. Successful therapy depends both on the skill of the therapist and your own willingness to examine difficult issues. Results can vary widely; nevertheless, when all factors are favorable, therapy can become an invaluable investment in your health and well-being.

Here are some criteria to evaluate when considering therapy:

- What you are looking for in yourself is the capacity to respond openly to life—and especially to your partner—without being severely pulled or limited by undertows from the past.
- You want to be able to experience your partner for the unique person she or he is, without blurring, confusing, or contaminating your current relationship with previous experiences with parent figures.
- You want to be able to chose as your partner someone who supports your growth as an individual.
- You want to be able to be appropriately responsive, trusting, sensitive, caring, and forgiving.
- You want to be able to create and experience intimacy—both sexually and emotionally.
- You want to be able to create and experience joy, aliveness, and satisfaction.

If you sense barriers within yourself that you are unable to tear down yourself and that prevent you from realizing these goals, therapy might help you improve the quality of your life.

SUMMARY

Apology and forgiveness can be two of the most difficult and valuable components of a world class marriage. But in order to be able to truly apologize and forgive, you may need to free yourself of shadowy connections from the past so that you can be alive to the present.

It's inevitable that you will say and do things that hurt each other's feelings. When you cause hurt, apologize. When you are apologized to, forgive. When either is difficult, review the principles in this chapter and work on your personal growth issues. The more you develop as a person, the greater your capacity for overcoming the difficulties that occur in any relationship and for creating the closeness of a world class marriage.

PILLAR 14

GROWING YOURSELF

Growth is the only evidence of life.

—John Henry Newman

"Grow up!" Patty's parents used to say during a fight when they were exasperated with each other. "You grow up yourself!" the other would retort. They were frustrated with each other and thought that the upset of the moment wouldn't have happened if the other had handled things more maturely. This is not exactly what we mean by "**growing yourself**." This chapter involves the extremely important challenge of developing yourself as a human being—primarily because of its importance in enhancing the quality of your life, and secondarily because it makes you a more desirable and interesting partner.

During the honeymoon phase, issues of personal development get pushed aside while each of you focuses on getting to know the other intimately, aided and abetted by sexual attraction and exploration. All cylinders are firing, and the relationship is infused with excitement. When that wears off, you are left with two flawed human beings who, hopefully, like and admire each other and have a commitment to work it out together. Still, something's missing—the wonderful energy charge of the honeymoon.

Nothing quite substitutes for that; it's uniquely powerful. Does this mean excitement in your relationship is gone forever? Certainly not, especially if you begin to look again at who you want to be in your life, what you want to do, and what your interests and goals are and begin to identify steps that continue your development as a curious and exciting person, bursting with vitality.

> Linda and Pete came to us to learn communication skills, but we soon learned that their sixteen-month relationship was near its end. Pete, who characterized himself as a very private person, felt "invaded" by Linda. He complained that she continually overstepped his boundaries. When Pete tried to share something personal with Linda, she was so eager to know more, to be of help, to have a sense of intimacy with Pete that she actually made it impossible for him to share with her. Eager to satisfy her own curiosity, she asked loads of questions, she probed him, and she urged him to talk by behaving seductively toward him—anything she could do to draw him out. She ultimately dominated all conversation. He responded to this by refusing to talk—erecting a barrier she could not cross. Feeling frustrated, Linda became even more determined to get through to Pete. These two people, both of whom actually wanted to share with each other, were so engaged in this strange battle that no intimate connection was actually made.

What's the solution to Linda and Pete's problems? Partially, it is to learn communication skills. Linda also must realize that Pete "owns" the conversation when he has something he wishes to share. Her role is to listen in a way that allows Pete to retain control of the conversation. But more importantly, Linda needs to develop herself as a person so that she feels a fuller sense of self, so that she has more going on for herself and within herself, so that she feels centered and whole, independent of Pete. As it was, she reached out in a needy, clinging way to connect with Pete, and he recoiled from this, making her even more desperate for connection. If she can find a meaningful way to grow herself and find deeper forms of satisfaction in her own life, she will be more self-contained and better able to respect Pete's boundaries. Ironically, this is likely to bring her more of the intimacy with her partner that she so desperately seeks.

Certainly, a strong and loving partnership itself goes a long way toward helping you feel good inside. Yet the more we as individuals are able to enrich our own lives, the more enabled we are to create an even stronger and more loving relationship with our partner. There is no substitute for growing yourself and enriching your own life.

Growing yourself is primarily about the importance of taking responsibility for creating a successful and satisfying life for yourself. Secondarily, but wonderfully, it is about being a full and interesting human being, continually attractive even to the person with whom you have lived for many years and who knows all your warts.

> Jessica and Matt have been together for eight years. She's recently joined a nonprofit organization working to promote international peace. This isn't one of Matt's interests, but he helps her with some computer graphics on the mailings she does for the organization. Jessica enjoys working with this organization because it introduces her to many interesting people and makes her feel she's doing something important. She also likes having this project to talk about with Matt.

> Jack's a retired policeman. Rather than stay home with nothing to do, he's joined two horticultural societies and is deeply involved with many aspects of gardening. He exhibits his flower arrangements and is an officer in both societies. Allison loves having his plants around the house, but more importantly, she loves having Jack involved in something that excites him.

Ralph likes to say that I get him "involved in the damndest things!" This includes hosting Japanese exchange students and a dinner party with a visiting French chef, shoveling piles of steer manure into the rose garden, throwing a party for the Chinese ambassador, studying Italian from cassette tapes, doing mailings for nonprofit organizations, and planning a family fiesta, to name just a few activities. There are more—and the fact that there are always things happening in our lives, many of which I bring about, is something that Ralph loves about me. Referring to them as the "damndest things" is his code for how much he enjoys the excitement.

Is Ralph the only one who likes this excitement? Of course not! I create these experiences primarily because they are of interest to me—so that I have a variety of things going on that are engaging, enriching, and satisfying. They are part of my continuous desire to grow myself and add spice to my own life. A by-product is that they make me feel alive.

ALIVENESS

Aliveness is an alluring quality. Yet, surprisingly, it hasn't been much discussed, either in professional or popular literature. We think this element deserves more attention because it nurtures the individual and excites the relationship.

Aliveness bespeaks a quality of openness, responsiveness, animation, and energy that is profoundly attractive to people. We believe in the importance of expanding your capacity to be alive to the richness, vastness, and excitement of life.

This vitality seems to be a prime quality to which we are attracted in others. We are captivated by the person with the vibrant smile, responsive emotions, and the ability to express thoughts and feelings with passion; the person open to new possibilities; the person with energy; the person putting effort into a worthy endeavor; the athlete overcoming big odds; the baby with the bright eyes and happy face. These all represent the quality of being vibrant and alive, and perhaps because it makes us feel more alive to experience this in another person, we are attracted to this quality in others. Therefore, we believe that keeping your own "aliveness quotient" high is an important aspect of keeping your relationship vital. And this is only possible when you see to it that your own basic needs get met.

> At eighteen, Hanna was tall, beautiful, and brilliant—full of life and promise. By age thirty, she had become the mother of three energetic boys and held a doctorate in biology. She was deeply unhappy in her marriage but felt she had to stay in the devastating relationship until her sons were grown. Expressing this frustration, she said, "It's only ten more years." When we saw her years later, she was a divorced alcoholic who had lost her prestigious job because of her drinking. She said that her life hadn't felt worth living for several years. Her spirit was crushed, and she looked twenty years older than her fifty-three years. Recently, our Christmas cards have been returned with an expired address notice, she's been identified as "missing" on our school roster, and we've come to fear the worst.

Hanna's story is poignant because it so vividly represents what we see as her "suicide of the spirit." Seeing no alternatives other than to stay in a painful relationship, she so completely sacrificed her own needs to those of her three boys that the only avenue for escape became alcohol. This downward spiral of discouragement, despair, and alcoholism, with its concomitant devastation of her career, eventually killed a precious part of her spirit and left her a broken shell of a person.

This is a terrible waste of a talented, worthwhile person and a tragedy for her family and friends. While Hanna was sensitive to her sons' needs, she failed to be sensitive to her own. Her story might have been different if she had somehow committed to finding ways to get her needs met and had kept her spirit alive rather than blunting her experience of life with excessive use of alcohol.

Keeping yourself in the game of life—vibrant and fully intact—is a task for each of us to take seriously. This entails being sensitive to your own needs, whatever they may be. You may have needs for challenges, for self-expression, for opportunity, for fun, for variety, for time alone, for time with others. Whatever your needs, you must find creative ways to meet them if you wish to keep your spirit alive. Of course, to keep your relationship flourishing at the same time requires that the solutions used to meet your needs are acceptable to your partner. If this should become an issue, it can be resolved through transparent sharing, empathic listening, and creative problem solving.

Cherishing your own aliveness and working to keep it nourished within the context of your marriage relationship is vital. It requires a purposeful commitment to your own needs as well as to your partner's. Ironically, for some people, protecting and nurturing your joyfulness, spontaneity, and openness to life may take a solemn and serious commitment. Think of your aliveness as something very precious that should not be allowed to become encrusted with the barnacles of discouragement and despair.

If the same old routines—the same television shows at the same times every night, the same vacation spot each year, the same route home every day—are stultifying your life; if stagnation and boredom are just around the corner; if your enthusiasm for life is waning and your growth is slowing, snap your eyelids open to the whole wide world that's out there and explore some new ways to become involved. Here's a tiny fraction of what's awaiting you: archaeology, art, music, languages, travel, photography, ecology, horticulture, entertaining, the stock market, sports, home improvement, stamp collecting, history, mathematics, writing, yoga, brainteasers, local theater productions, chess, health, volunteer opportunities, world peace, household pets, growing organic food, literary programs, community activities, reading for the blind, volunteering for nonprofits, going back to school, personal enrichment classes, church activities, astronomy, Sister Cities programs, poetry, preserving the environment, sailing, urban cleanup campaigns, helping seniors, rural poverty programs, literacy programs, exploring the Internet, teaching relationship skills classes—the list is endless!

Getting Involved

It is often said that it's important to "get involved in something that's bigger than yourself." The reasons given for this include the value of having a big challenge or something that puts your life into perspective. Being engaged in a worthwhile activity takes your focus off the pettiness of daily concerns, stretches your intellectual limits, expands your belief in your own capabilities, and nurtures your self-esteem. All of this helps you grow into a more complex, capable, and sensitive person who is more satisfying to yourself and more satisfying to your partner as well. You both benefit from living in this enriched environment.

A secondary benefit of having compelling outside interests is that they take pressure off the primary relationship. When you look to your partner for everything, you surely will be disappointed. No relationship can meet all your needs. Recognizing this by developing interesting but non-competing outside interests lightens the burden on your relationship.

Growing Yourself Psychologically

Both experts and laypeople alike espouse the value of "working on your marriage," and although it sounds sensible, we have come to believe that it isn't marriages that need the work. Clearly, it is important to learn communication and relationship skills, since they enable you to avoid many of the pitfalls and unintentional wounds that occur from unskillful behaviors. Beyond that, we believe that the most effective way to work on your marriage is to work on your self—the best way to create real progress in your marriage is through the process of personal growth.

When you can connect with yourself, know how to communicate authentically with your partner, and listen deeply to your partner, you are able to connect with each other's humanity. This intimacy is the most fertile soil for a relationship. Personal growth enables you to know yourself and, simultaneously, to see your partner as very much the same as yourself—as a worthy human being with similar needs, desires, and magnificence.

The most effective foundation for personal growth—either in yourself or another—is created through empathy, acceptance, and genuineness, which promote growth in all relationships. Over time, these conditions create a climate that allows for self-knowledge to unfold, for the healing of hurts, for the softening of rough edges, for the release of defensiveness and self-defeating behaviors, for the development of self, and for the sense of being who you are meant to be.

DEFENSIVENESS

Among the many threats to intimacy and personal growth that couples face is one whose pervasiveness is seldom discussed: **defensiveness**. Defensiveness is the behavior of covering up, explaining, or otherwise protecting ourselves when we perceive attack or criticism, a characteristic all too common among human beings.

Defensiveness develops in childhood largely through our interaction with parents who try to shape us into properly socialized human beings and who have a strong desire for peace and predictability. To accomplish these goals, parents teach, give orders, threaten, blame, scold, interrogate, moralize, analyze, criticize, and utilize various other attempts to control the unpredictable little blobs of protoplasm they are raising. Because of these somewhat clumsy behavior-shaping attempts, most of us end up feeling pushed around as children—controlled, misunderstood, and perhaps inadequate. Because these affronts to our self-esteem were difficult to tolerate, we developed the tactic of explaining, justifying, and defending our actions in the hopes that our parents' anger would subside and they would think well of us. We learned how to mount a successful defense, and defensiveness quickly became an ingrained habit. Moreover, we are likely to have also modeled our parents' behavior-molding techniques, and our manifestation of these same behaviors now readily provoke defensiveness in our partner. This simple, classic story illustrates defensiveness in action: there was a strong earthquake and the worried mother called out to her little son, "Peter, where are you?" The six-year old replied, "I didn't do it, Mommy!"

Our parents' techniques were learned at their parents' knees, and it's helpful to have compassion for the strain parents are under while trying to educate, tolerate, and socialize their offspring during the long years of childhood. Nevertheless, a residue of these years—defensiveness—can be a difficult characteristic that remains part of our personality, despite the fact that we no longer have any reasonable or understandable fear of parental criticism or rejection. This defensiveness persists whenever we feel we are in a situation that seems threatening—when we perceive the other person has no empathy for us, is not accepting of us, or is not being genuine. Perceiving some form of danger, we respond defensively: we misinterpret their communication to match our fears, move into a controlling mode for damage control, lose our empathy and acceptance for the other person, and our own genuineness takes a backseat to tactical considerations. Unfortunately, these conditions tend to create defensiveness in our partner and a vicious circle quickly results. This is called marital discord.

If you've been together for a while, it's likely you've seen defensiveness in your partner—explanations or excuses designed to protect him- or herself in situations where it wasn't necessary, because he or she wasn't actually being criticized. You have the advantage of knowing that you weren't going to attack your partner and cause psychological damage, so you can easily spot your partner's unnecessary defensiveness. Yet your partner behaved as if it was about to happen. Under these circumstances, it's possible to observe how demeaning it is for your partner to scramble for justification of his or her behavior in the face of an ally. Observing your partner's defensiveness, you recognize how unnecessary, time-consuming, demeaning, and diverting it is from what you are trying to accomplish together. You may even have felt impatient listening to your partner's unnecessary defensiveness sometimes.

John Gottman's research with couples at the University of Washington identified defensiveness as one of the key factors that cause damage to the marital relationship. Defensiveness, he says, "can lead to endless spirals of negativity. By finding the courage not to be defensive (or at least recognizing and minimizing it as much as possible,) your marriage will almost certainly improve."[7]

What Creates Defensiveness?

Defensiveness is a product of the two people involved—the sender and the listener. It is evident that the listener is involved in its creation, because it is the listener who responds defensively. Yet, in all cases, the behavior of the sender is also an integral triggering factor, whether to a small or large extent. It is less important to determine who is more responsible for creating defensiveness than it is for both parties to work on minimizing its recurrence in the relationship. In some respects, defensiveness is like a gopher in the yard: regardless of whether it comes from your neighbor's property or from your own, both gardens are threatened.

The defensive person hears something she or he perceives to be a threat and takes action to ward off anticipated damage. Besides talking about the subject at hand, the defensive person also says things he or she thinks will bolster his image in the eyes of the other—things he or she thinks will allow him or her to win, dominate, impress, escape punishment, and avoid or lessen a perceived or anticipated attack.

In some situations, defensiveness arises in response to circumstances that are reminiscent of a painful experience that occurred in a previous relationship. These situations are common in a marriage, as one's spouse often becomes inseparably linked on an unconscious level with one's parents and authority figures from childhood. It may not take much from our partner to trigger an overreaction based on such a situation. A certain tone of voice, a look, a certain word, and we're transported back to a painful situation twenty, thirty, forty years ago when we were hurt, criticized, humiliated. We overreact to the present because of the past. We defend ourselves at all costs and engage in defensiveness far out of proportion to the current, actual threat. In such a situation, our spouse may feel like an involuntary player in this one-person drama and wonder, "What did I do?"

Low self-esteem can play an important role in generating defensiveness. When we have pockets of low self-esteem, it doesn't take much from our partner—maybe just a sigh that has nothing to do with us personally—to cause us to feel threatened and act defensively. Low self-esteem rears its ugly head in many unexpected places, and it often plays a key role in defensiveness.

Defensive Climates

In some situations, defensiveness is a response to behavior that almost everyone would perceive as threatening. No matter how self-assured and unscarred one partner is, the other says and does things that make defensiveness nearly inevitable.

Jack Gibb's work on defensiveness at the National Training Laboratories identified six behaviors that stimulate defensiveness and six that reduce defensiveness.[8] What stimulates defensiveness, along with some examples, appears in the following box.

STIMULATORS OF A DEFENSIVE CLIMATE

Evaluation: Speech or nonverbal behavior that appears evaluative or judgmental—blame, moral judgments, good/bad evaluations, questioning one's motives.

"That wasn't a very smart move."

"If you hadn't signed that stupid contract, we wouldn't be in such a jam!"

Control: Speech or nonverbal behavior that attempts to control the other.

"I'm not going to allow my wife to dress like that!"

"You so much as look at another woman and you'll be sorry."

Strategy: Being perceived as being engaged in a stratagem involving ambiguous or multiple motivations.

"I am managing the money and everything is under control."

"I was with some friends, and it's none of your business."
Neutrality: Speech with low affect that communicates little warmth, caring, or concern for the other's welfare.
"Whatever you say."
"I really don't care one way or the other."
Superiority: Any verbal or nonverbal behavior that communicates to the other that she or he feels superior in position, power, wealth, intellectual ability, physical characteristics, or other ways.
"I'm handling the matter and I don't need any interference from you."
"Maybe if you'd bothered to finish your education you'd understand what I'm saying."
Certainty: Appearing to know the answer, to require no additional data, to regard oneself as teacher rather than partner, being dogmatic.
"You'd better mark my words, because if you keep forgetting to click on 'Save,' you're going to have a disaster!"
"My mind's made up, and there's no question about it!"

Supportive Climates

The best way to avoid defensiveness lies in creating a "supportive climate" for yourself and your partner. Gibb's research identifies six antidotes to defensiveness, which are listed, along with some examples, in the following box.

STIMULATORS OF A SUPPORTIVE CLIMATE

Description (vs. Evaluation): Descriptive, non-blameful speech.
"I'm afraid that move will cause problems for us."
"It looks like that contract turned out to be terribly unfavorable to us, and I'm quite unhappy about it."
Problem Orientation (vs. Control): Communicating a desire to collaborate and creating a problem orientation, which implies no predetermined solution, attitude, or method that will be imposed.

"I'm afraid you'll create the wrong impression with that dress. Would you consider another outfit?"

"I know you love to flirt at parties, but it makes me feel so insecure. How could we handle this situation better?"

Spontaneity (vs. Strategy): Appearing spontaneous and free of deception.

"Managing the money is a little scary for me, and I'm afraid I get a bit rigid. But tell me your concerns and I'll try to calm down."

"After work, two guys from the office and I stopped at the bar for a drink, and I guess I was afraid you wouldn't approve."

Empathy (vs. Neutrality): Conveying empathy for the feelings and respect for the worth of the other.

"Sounds like you really feel strongly about that. Help me understand that better."

"It seems like this is a hard decision for you. Would you like to talk about it some more?"

Equality (vs. Superiority): Being willing to enter into participative planning with mutual trust and respect.

"Let's think through what our financial priorities are."

"Let me see if I can make my thinking on this clearer."

Provisionalism (vs. Certainty): Being willing to experiment with behavior, attitudes, and ideas; communicating that the other may have some control over the outcome.

"Maybe if I get off your back about 'saving' all the time, you'll figure it out in your own way."

"I feel pretty strongly about this, but maybe I'm too close to the issue. What are your thoughts?"

REDUCING YOUR OWN DEFENSIVENESS

Defensiveness is often an impulsive, unplanned reaction that is hard to prevent. It helps to work on becoming conscious of the various ways we express our defensiveness so that we can start to observe it, either while it's happening or soon afterward. If we can observe our own behavior without blame (with empathy and acceptance for ourselves), this helps release the grip that defensiveness has on our unconscious, eventually allowing us to become less defensive as well as less fearful and controlling.

If you consciously know that your partner doesn't intend to threaten you, but you notice defensiveness in yourself, gently remind yourself that your partner doesn't intend to make you defensive; your partner wishes you to feel safe. Remind yourself that you don't need to explain, justify, or excuse your behavior—that you're a worthy person always working at the best level you can manage, even though it is not always acceptable to others. Recognize that defensiveness isn't necessary or beneficial and that it subtly demeans your self-esteem and creates unnecessary flotsam in the relationship with your partner. Consciously choose not to defend yourself whenever you become aware of it as an option; find the strength to forgo defensiveness.

By experiencing moments of undefended vulnerability, you will have the opportunity to learn to trust in the safety of your relationship with your partner. These scary moments of intimacy—undefended moments with your partner—open the door to greater psychological health and a profound sense of closeness. Both you and your partner will experience many desirable side effects through your work in reducing your own defensiveness. Besides an increased freedom from your own defensive feelings, you will be able to bring increased amounts of empathy, acceptance, and genuineness to the relationship as a result of your work spent on growing these conditions within yourself. As you engage in the process of reducing your defensiveness through observation, empathy, and self-acceptance, you become more *yourself*, you become more of a person for your partner to enjoy. This path toward continuous growth as a person is an important ingredient in creating a deep and rich relationship with your partner.

SUMMARY

Popular magazines are filled with tantalizing tips on how to improve yourself—to be more beautiful, handsome, sexy, strong, slim, and better in bed—so you can be a happier person, catch a mate, or continue to excite the one you have. The success of these magazines attests to the widespread belief—or perhaps, hope—that skin-deep solutions will achieve those profound goals. This is generally not the case.

Growing yourself as an individual is the real route toward becoming a happy and fulfilled person, and one who continues to excite your spouse. This includes expanding your talents, capacities, perspectives on life, and your depth and humanity as a person, as well as learning to reduce your own defensiveness and create a climate that helps reduce defensiveness in your partner. Your personal depth and vitality are major keys to developing and maintaining your own world class marriage.

15

PILLAR 15

FORGING A BOND

Chains do not hold a marriage together. It is threads, hundreds of tiny threads, which sew people together through the years.

—Simone Signoret

Years ago, a professional colleague contrasted our marriage with his, saying, "The big thing about the two of you is that you have bonded." We knew intuitively what he meant—that independent of conscious commitment or rational thoughts about the reasons for staying in the relationship, we had somehow become psychologically glued together and were going to stay that way. No matter what difficulties and upsets we have with each other, ending the relationship is never a serious option for either of us.

We became interested in the concept of **bonding**, even though we couldn't define it clearly, weren't sure what created it, and didn't know if it was always desirable (what if it locked you into a terrible relationship?). Bonding seems very valuable for us, and we see the ingredients that have a good chance of fostering it, but we'll say clearly: if from the bottom of your heart, you know the relationship is bad for you, don't lock yourself into it! We offer the concept to people in good relationships as a strengthening enrichment to a world class marriage.

The dictionary has some enlightening definitions:

Bond (*noun*): Something that unites individuals or peoples; something that binds or fastens; a cementing material that holds abrasive grains together; the strong and enduring quality of affection.

Bond (*verb*): To join; to hold together or solidify by means of a bond or binder; to cause to adhere firmly.

These definitions apply quite well to the concept as we experience it. The value we get from bonding is the confidence in the long-term survival of our relationship—the sense that we no longer need to waste time and psychological energy on escapist fantasies or abandonment worries and can focus on living our lives and dealing with life from the safety of an unusually stable relationship.

How do couples become bonded? Some do this through a baptism of fire—successfully weathering a serious problem or disaster together during which they are able to keep their heart-to-heart connection intact. In retrospect, we believe that a disastrous job loss early in our relationship played an important part in our bonding—our disguised good fortune, as it turned out. For others, we believe it is possible to consciously create conditions that foster bonding, helping them to create their own glue. We see five main "bonding ingredients":

- your intention to commit fully to the relationship;
- conscious use of the 16 Pillars;
- engaging in "in-it-together" activities;
- surrendering anticommitment defenses; and
- living together through life's crucible over time.

INTENTIONS

What are your **intentions** toward this relationship? Do you intend to make it work with this partner? Are you committed to this relationship emotionally? Is this person your beloved? Is this person truly precious to you? Are you really *in* the relationship?

If your answer to any of these questions is "no," then it is doubtful that your intentionality is strong enough to create a bond. If your answer is "yes," then you are already creating the glue that keeps a relationship together.

USING THE PILLARS

With the conscious intention to be in a committed relationship, the use of the 16 Pillars of a world class marriage becomes a powerful tool with which to foster bonding and strengthening every aspect of your relationship. The pillars provide shared understanding about behaviors that damage relationships and how to avoid them, as well as understanding about behaviors that strengthen relationships and how to use them. Aside from their many other advantages, using these pillars is a vital element in creating the conditions in which bonding can occur.

IN-IT-TOGETHER BEHAVIORS

A third ingredient for bonding seems to be choosing activities that foster the sense of being "in it" together. This enhances the sense of sharing your lives with each other. Such behaviors could include, for example, attending your partner's "big occasions," sharing money and other possessions, doing things to help your partner, going to the gym together, and "owning" your involvement in your partner's circumstances (e.g., speaking from the point of view of "I can't come because I want to take care of my sick wife," rather than "I can't come because my wife is sick"). Of course, each of you will have separate interests and activities, but be aware of the need for a strong balance of in-it-together activities if fostering a bond is your goal.

An attitude of "in-it togetherness" is also valuable during difficult times. For example, when a visiting relative does things that irritate, it's important that both of you, perhaps especially for the unrelated partner, get the chance to vent to each other about the visitor's annoying behavior and to be listened to with empathic acceptance. Even though this may be your own mother, brother, or other relative, listening empathically to your mate's hurts and frustrations about them is much more productive than defending your kin's actions. At such times, disengage yourself from a sense of family loyalty and allow your partner to express to you his or her annoyance or hurt. To deny this causes your partner to feel abandoned at a critical time.

This doesn't mean taking sides or confronting the relative over the offensive remark or behavior—that is the task of the offended party, if it seems necessary. Your job is simply to offer a receptive ear. All that is asked for and needed is empathic acceptance, which at times of stress heightens the sense of being in it together. You may also discover how nice it is to have you partner share similar experiences you've long had with your own family.

Another vital and long-term area in which it is imperative to develop the sense of being in it together is child rearing. This is a twenty-year process, continually bringing challenges and stresses along with deep rewards, and parenting is often marked by disagreements, large and small, regarding the best way to proceed. It's easy to allow child care disagreements to drive a wedge between you and your partner. See chapter 19, "Kids and the Relationship," for a more complete discussion of this issue.

To maintain the sense of being in it together as parents, keep in mind the idea that raising your child is something that the two of you have chosen to do within the context of your relationship. It is a shared, long-term activity in which each of you may have different responsibilities and challenges, and each of you has your own separate relationships with the child. But it is a task you share together as no one else on earth does: the responsibility for bringing your children into the world and for helping them achieve successful adulthood. In this context of profound sharing, you need to know that when the problems seem too tough to bear you can go to your partner and find an empathic ear. It's comforting to know that differences over parenting styles won't stand in the way of a good listen when things go wrong. When empathic acceptance is always available, you can experience the benefits of being in it together, and the various trials of parenting will only strengthen your bond.

SURRENDERING YOUR ANTICOMMITMENT DEFENSES

Probably the greatest barrier to becoming truly bonded and enjoying all the benefits that flow from that is the need of one or both partners to secretly keep their options open: "Maybe my partner will change, then I'll commit"; "Maybe someone better will come along"; or "Maybe I'll get hurt if I'm too vulnerable." These **anticommitment defenses** represent understandable fears and fantasies, but they result in secretly withholding a "final" commitment. They insert an inch (or mile) of distance between the two of you that makes bonding difficult.

If your best judgment tells you this is indeed a relationship worth elevating to world class status, you must find the courage to surrender these defenses. Somehow, you must say to yourself and freely acknowledge to your partner, "I am committed to this relationship no matter what. Regardless of what happens, I have burned my bridges!" I can still remember when Ralph first said this to me, and it still makes my heart tingle.

Surrendering your avenue of escape is one of life's major gambles, even though the risks are small in a good relationship. And the payoff can be huge. Removing that last inch of distance can be transforming for a relationship, making it safe to love at a depth far greater than before and eliminating the final impediment to becoming truly bonded.

TIME

Time works a kind of magic on a good relationship. Time combines with the first four ingredients to create a transformed sense of state. Time shared and problems faced in the complex crucible of life forge a profound sense of truly belonging to each other. Building shared experiences, shared space, and shared lives creates a depth to the relationship that is profound and irreplaceable.

IS BONDING FOR EVERYONE?

Bonding is a special state of commitment and identification with another person reserved only for a deep relationship grounded in love and trust.

Therefore, our best advice in relation to bonding is to love wisely—don't rush in and make a commitment that goes beyond the reality of what you really have together. Get to know the person you are with and develop trust and emotional intimacy over a period of time. And when you know that the relationship is right for you, that you deeply love and trust your partner, and that you trust in your shared capacity to solve problems together successfully, let the other shoe drop. Lay down the rest of your emotional defenses and truly open yourself to this other person. Surrender to a shared future. Make it your intention to succeed together, commit to using the 16 Pillars, and allow time to bond you in a world class marriage.

(16)

PILLAR 16

NURTURING THE HONEYMOON

We don't believe in rheumatism and true love until after the first attack.

—Marie von Ebner-Eschenbach

A world class marriage, like a beautiful garden, thrives on nourishment. During the honeymoon phase of a relationship, it's common for both partners to engage in any number of romantic behaviors. Post-honeymoon, this tends to drop off dramatically. This is like fertilizing a garden while the plants are young and expecting them to thrive and bloom forever on that one round of fertilizer. Plants decline on such a regimen and so do marriages. Like all beautiful gardens, a marriage that is regularly nourished—in this case, with loving words and deeds—blooms gloriously and nurtures the closeness that keeps your special honeymoon feelings alive.

American feminist author Ursula Le Guin notes that "Love just doesn't sit there like a stone. It has to be made, like bread, remade all the time, made new."

How can you nourish the honeymoon and make new the relationship? You know how! It's like exercising—just do it—with words and deeds.

DEEDS

There are lots of ways to nurture the honeymoon feelings in your relationship, and as action sometimes speaks louder than words, deeds are an important form of relationship nourishment. The options are limited only by your creativity. Some ideas include love notes, walks along the beach, pet names, loving, sexy, or playful glances, bouquets of flowers, chocolates, silly gifts, sexy gifts, special surprises, an hour away from the kids, watching television holding hands, back rubs, foot massages, playful tickling, showering together, pushing each other on a swing at the park, lying under the stars, date nights, candlelit dinner in the bedroom, dancing, champagne, romantic vacations—anything that allows you to communicate and experience the joy you feel about your relationship with your partner.

HEART-SHAPED WORDS

Positive I-Messages, or **heart-shaped words**, are a powerful way to communicate your love, admiration, and caring verbally. These messages contain the word "I" followed by a verb that describes your feeling about your partner. The classic is "I love you," which seems to have an equivalent in every language. Perhaps this is because human beings, regardless of culture, thrive on simple, strong expressions of our importance to other human beings. World class marriages are nurtured by positive I-Language.

Here's a tip in crafting some heart-shaped words: rather than describing your partner—"You are beautiful"; "You are so smart"; "You are wonderful"—use I-Language to describe something internal within yourself. These messages are expressions of yourself. To be meaningful, positive I-Messages must be honest expressions of how you think or feel. They cannot be based on flattery or lies. Remember the importance of genuineness.

Because they are about you, the sender, and because they are grounded in the reality of your feelings, they have a real advantage over standard compliments such as, "You're so beautiful." Your partner might quickly brush this compliment aside by saying, "Oh, my hair looks terrible," if your statement doesn't match her self-image or it feels immodest to agree. But by saying it in the form of a communication about what's going on in *you* in regard to something about your partner—for example, "I love the way you look"—it is easier for your partner to take it in and benefit from it (perhaps by thinking internally, "You do? Oh, wow!"). Since positive I-Language is a true statement about your feelings, your partner is less likely to negate it and more likely to enjoy and be nurtured by it.

Positive I-Language is varied and these expressions can be rich, satisfying, even dazzling:

"I am committed to you and I want our relationship to work."
"I adore you."
"I am turned on by you like crazy."
"I go for you."
"I love the way you smell."
"I love to feel you."
"I love to make love to you."
"I want to fill your life with flowers."
"I am yours."
"I love the way your mind works."
"I want you."
"I am yours forever."
"I adore your face."
"I love to touch your hands."
"I'm so impressed with the way you handled that."
"I love to look at you."
"I love to hear you talk."
"I love to see the way you are with others."
"I am fascinated by you."
"I admire you."
"I love being your husband/wife/partner."
"I feel lucky to be married to you."
"I really like you."
"I go for you big time."
"I don't know what I did to deserve you."
"I adore everything about you."

"I am deeply happy with you."

"I'm the luckiest person in the world to be with you."

VULNERABILITY

Sometimes people hesitate to send messages expressing their vulnerability, either for fear of seeming somehow too much in love or too vulnerable or for fear of upsetting the emotional balance of your relationship by expressing your profound commitment and love for your partner, thus giving your partner the "upper hand." In a committed relationship these notions are balderdash.

First of all, it is important to recognize that vulnerability is the name of the game when it comes to love. You cannot love someone without being vulnerable. Love is a vulnerable feeling—it is not a protected position. And what makes love so precious is its tenderness. Human beings respond to tenderness, to vulnerability, to cute babies, to kittens, to puppy dogs, and most of all, to expressions of love. If you are going to be able to express love, you have to make peace with knowing that it is an expression of vulnerability.

Second, nothing is as well received as messages of love, admiration, and caring in your love relationship. Rather than upsetting the emotional balance, these messages are bonding. Imagine, for example, one day hearing your beloved escalate his or her message from the standard "I love you" to "I adore you." What does that do to you? Do you say to yourself, "Aha! Now I can really get away with murder!"? No, what you are likely to feel is bliss and contentment—a bath of profound emotional safety. This kind of security has wonderful effects on people, bringing out our best qualities as human beings.

Such positive self-disclosure is a cost-free and satisfying way to reach out to your partner and nourish the honeymoon feelings in your relationship. Look for every opportunity to nurture your relationship by sharing your admiring and loving thoughts and feelings with your partner this way.

Be generous with your affection—never withhold it. Be forthcoming about communicating how special your partner is to you. You could do this by buying your beloved an expensive diamond—a code many women understand and respond to well—or you can do this with the budget of a pauper and the heart of a poet. The only requirement is the desire to reach your partner with the message that she or he is deeply special to you.

TARGETED IMPACT

Focus on your partner's preferences so that your caring has meaningful impact. If your partner loves flowers, focus on flowers; if your partner needs a break, escape for a day away together; if your partner enjoys poetry, get out the paper; if your partner responds to lovemaking, put on the romantic music (see chapter 10, "Giving Caring the Way It Matters"). Often people give what they want to give rather than what their partner wants. The best way to nurture the honeymoon feelings is to give what your partner wants. Put yourself in your partner's shoes. Recall things you have heard your partner say she or he wants and offer that. If your own ideas seem inadequate, consult a book. Gregory Godek's *1,001 Ways to Be Romantic* (see bibliography) is a fountainhead of creative ideas. What partner wouldn't thrill to learn that his or her beloved consulted a book in order to expand his or her ability to express feelings of love? Be blatant about your commitment to nourish the relationship with your beloved. Take seriously the idea that your marriage, like all living things, needs the equivalent of food, water, sunshine, and tender loving care to flourish. Pump expressions of your love into your relationship and watch it blossom.

II

APPLYING THE PILLARS

Every couple's relationship is unique, with special bonds of closeness and special difficulties and tensions. The 16 Pillars are universally applicable. Nevertheless, some relationships have characteristics and issues that we feel demand special discussion. We present these thoughts in the following five chapters.

17

LIVING TOGETHER

The bonds that unite another person to ourself exist only in our mind.

—Marcel Proust

Unmarried couples living together, once a rarity, are common in today's world, and these relationships run the gamut from experimental flings to long-term committed partnerships. For some couples, getting married never has been and never will be an option. They live together, make their lives together, are fully committed to their relationship, and are accepted by family and friends as such. For whatever reasons—and there can be many—these couples have no interest in becoming legally married.

Other couples fall into living together right after they fall into bed together. They wake up to discover they are together with an "as long as we both feel like it" understanding. For many of these unions, the end of the honeymoon finds one of them out the door for good.

For still other couples, living together is a step along the road to marriage, a kind of precommitment. After dating awhile and finding their relationship growing, they decide to try living together, usually on an exclusive basis—a sort of premarriage to test the waters. If all goes well, they eventually marry.

Living together represents something different for each couple involved. The levels of connection and commitment can range from very low to very high. Because no public vows of commitment are exchanged, it is not readily apparent to outsiders what these relationships mean to the people involved; some may have a clear understanding about the meaning of the relationship, others may be almost entirely in the dark.

Benjamin and Melanie knew each other since college. After graduation, they moved to New York and took an apartment together. At times they are lovers; at other times they both see others and live together just as roommates. Both are happy with this way of living together—sharing expenses and some parts of their lives while maintaining separateness from each other in other areas. After some puzzlement, their parents have become cautiously accepting of this unusual arrangement.

Jenny and Jack got together after they had both been married before— she after a brief marriage, and Jack after a twenty-year marriage followed by a short second marriage. They met at work and developed a friendship that slowly turned into a romance. After living together for a few months, Jenny wanted to get married. Although Jack loved her, he was unable to make the commitment to another marriage. This was hard for Jenny, but she agreed to back down from pressuring him for it. After five years of living together, when Jack felt "married" emotionally, he was able to make their commitment legal.

Yussul and Sasha merged their households and children from two previous marriages into a fully blended family—moving to a new city together, purchasing a house, sharing holidays with all of their children, helping with the care of their aging parents. They never married and always said they never planned to, but all their friends knew them to be a fully committed couple. To everyone's surprise, they decided to celebrate their twenty-fifth anniversary of living together by getting married. Their charming wedding invitations said they "got a bad case of can't stop loving you!"

Kent and Alexa have known each other since school and have lived together for fourteen years. They both have busy lives with full-time careers and many other activities and have decided that they don't have time for children. They are a close couple, but since having children is not in their future, they never plan to marry. Their parents are disappointed not to expect grandchildren but have fully accepted their union.

While two of these couples eventually married, the other two probably won't, and in this present age, they will pay little if any penalty for what was stridently called "living in sin" in earlier times. This is fortunate for them, because making a long-term relationship work is difficult enough without the added burden of social disapproval. How did those who once "lived in sin" become socially acceptable "significant others"?

From ancient times until sometime in the past century, we lived in a predominantly agrarian society where the principal means of livelihood was farming. The only inheritable wealth was land, males were generally the only beneficiary, there was no effective contraception, and a child born out of wedlock and its mother were virtually condemned to beggary. This resulted in the need for an extremely rigid social order to guarantee proper rights of inheritance and social class. The institution that guaranteed this was marriage. To make it all work, marriage had to be sacrosanct and inviolate. The church added its endorsement to this important social union, increasing the sense of its importance for all.

Because of astounding changes in the past hundred years—including the shift from an agricultural society to the industrial era to the information age, along with the development of effective contraception—a wide array of jobs and careers have opened up, women are no longer pigeonholed as baby-makers and have achieved basic parity with men, and the need for rigid lines of succession has vanished. With it have vanished the economic and social imperatives that demanded traditional marriage, and the disapproval of divorce and of living together unmarried has greatly dissipated. But new freedoms have brought new challenges. For couples who choose not to marry, what substitute for marriage vows are available to keep them together and give their lives meaning? Interestingly, the answers seem to be the same as those that give the best marriages meaning and longevity—close, caring relationships and deep commitment. As ever, each couple must conduct their own search for these.

WORKING OUT THE RELATIONSHIP

For some couples, the lack of a marriage vow signifies that they have not yet articulated together the meaning of their relationship. Many couples find it difficult to talk about such matters, and for them it seems easier to "just live together" and hope that somehow everything works out okay.

Others are afraid of making a commitment to marriage or simply don't ever want to be married, and for them, living together seems a safer, easier option. Although this may eliminate some legal complications, it does not eliminate any of the essential relationship issues nor the importance of communication for building a successful relationship.

One good sign that the process of building a relationship has begun is when you find yourselves talking about it. For some young people, when this occurs, it marks the transition to "serious" dating. For those who are casually living together, a sign that you have become a couple is that your relationship becomes a topic of conversation. In fact, until discussions of your relationship develop, you are probably less a "couple" than "friends with privileges."

For relationships to work successfully, whether married or not, the partners need to explore, discuss, and develop a body of common understandings about their relationship. Ideally, this is an evolving, ongoing process with new understandings and clarifications articulated as feelings change over time. Staying current about your relationship with your partner is an important ingredient of a successful relationship.

When unmarried couples explore and learn how they both feel about issues such as their importance to each other, the strength of their affection and love, what role they now play and want to play in each other's lives in the future, and what hopes and expectations they have for their future together, the resulting clarifications benefit the relationship. Even if their feelings for each other are not fully developed or articulated, this kind of sharing builds trust in each other and confidence in the union. Without it, the relationship may suffer. Furthermore, false expectations and serious misunderstandings can lie hidden and result in painful missteps and hurt feelings later.

Probably the most vulnerable to these dangers are young unmarried couples who are afraid their relationship will not survive a close look and tacitly decide to hope for the best rather than open the subject for discussion. Ultimately, "the best" would be mustering the courage to uncover the facts before investing more of their lives in a relationship grounded in vagueness and uncertainty. If they find nothing of substance there, they can move on to more promising partners. If they find a real basis for staying together, they will have started the invaluable process of building a meaningful future together.

SPECIAL PROBLEMS OF LIVING TOGETHER

As society has loosened its moral restraints on unmarried couples living together, it has become a much more frequent occurrence. In 1960, only about 500,000 unmarried couples lived together in the United States; by 2000, that number increased to 5,000,000. Currently, about two-thirds of American couples live together before they marry. This has been fueled both by the ease of living together in today's society and the desire of many young couples to avoid horrific problems associated with divorce, which many of them have witnessed firsthand. Consequently, many couples live together as a way to test the relationship for its marriage readiness, and others do so specifically to avoid the trauma of divorce.

But cohabitation itself is far from being risk free. Although at first glance it seems that living together reduces the risks associated with divorce, the percentage of cohabiting couples who break up is higher than for married ones, even in European countries where cohabiting is fully accepted as a legal partnership.[9] Although cohabiting breakups may be easier on some than divorce, cohabiting is not a solution that avoids all the hardships associated with divorce, and in fact it may undermine commitment, which is increasingly being seen as crucial for relationship success. Ironically, as couples have come to see living together as an easy way to have the benefits of marriage without its baggage, they may be undermining their chances for success by not recognizing the importance of intentionality and commitment as essential components for achieving the relationship happiness they seek.

With the apparent ease of living together, the critical factor overlooked is the predictable end of the relationship's honeymoon—when the rose-colored glasses come off and each partner sees the other's flaws and understands the specific complications of the relationship. This time comes in every relationship, married or not. How you handle your relationship's issues together as they come to light determines whether the relationship succeeds in the long run or not. Without a commitment to making it work together, it's easy for couples to close the door on the relationship. "Good-bye. Good luck. See you around." And on to the next one, without learning anything beneficial about what it takes to make any relationship succeed.

Commitment

A particular stress on the cohabiting relationship is that it exists without any expressions of commitment. This leaves the door open for one partner to leave when there is upset or conflict, which creates fear and vulnerability in the other partner, as well as a climate of instability within the relationship. Making and receiving a genuine commitment to the relationship is therefore an important ingredient in creating stability and satisfaction, whether you are married or not.

However, many people have trouble making that commitment. Sometimes this reflects an underlying questioning of or dissatisfaction with the relationship. For others happy in their relationship, commitment problems stem from a particular fear of feeling trapped—"What if this doesn't work out?" "What if somebody better comes along?" "What if I find I just want to be free?" These folks—more often men than women—have not yet learned the truth of the saying, "Nothing ventured, nothing gained." As with everything else in life, there certainly are no guarantees in relationships, but you have to play to win.

A stumbling block for others is misunderstanding what a commitment is, seeing it as a promise to your partner, creating an obligation along the lines of, "for better for worse, for richer, for poorer, in sickness and in health," a time-honored excerpt from traditional marriage vows. True commitment, however, is separate from marriage vows per se. A commitment is an internal pledge made to yourself that you intend to honor, in this case that you will be true to your beloved, that you are henceforth devoted to this other person and this relationship and to successfully working it out together. It is, in fact, a promise made to *yourself*, not to your partner. When you voice this important commitment to your partner, its public declaration strengthens your resolve to keep it. And knowing of your pledge builds closeness and trust in your mate.

Such a self-promise is connected to your integrity, and thus it becomes an important component of the way you view yourself. Therefore, honoring your commitment to your relationship with your partner is an essential part of your self-esteem. To violate that is to violate your own ability to trust in yourself. It is central to your deepest feelings about yourself. Thus, committing to a relationship is a major step in your growth as a responsible and fully functioning person, not to mention its importance in cementing the relationship with your partner.

Couples who live together with high levels of acceptance, understanding, and commitment have strong, marriage-like relationships. Those who live together without these ingredients risk significant problems once the honeymoon comes to a close. As things settle down and illusion turns into vivid reality, the work of relationship building is as vital to an unmarried couple's happiness as it is to those who are married. And because there is no legally binding commitment to each other, it can be argued that the work of relationship building may be even more essential for unmarried couples.

APPLYING THE PILLARS

The following pillars may be especially useful for unmarried couples who are living together.

Pillar 1: Setting Goals

Since living together lacks the legal, religious, and social symbols and trappings of a traditional marriage, articulating your shared and agreed-upon goals for the relationship and for yourselves as individuals can provide beneficial and much-needed structure. This can be especially useful in new relationships where there may not have been much discussion and agreement about goals. Articulating and working on shared and agreed-upon goals help propel a couple's thoughts into the future, giving more reality to the idea of continuing a life together and raising both partners' confidence that the union will last.

Pillar 4: Using Power Listening

Power listening is especially beneficial for new couples to help them get to know each other at a deeper level and make contact with the needs, wants, fears, hopes, dreams, and humanity of the other. It is even more valuable as the wave of happy hormones during the honeymoon begins to subside and the inevitable human flaws in your partner begin to appear. Power listening and power listening lite are the windows into your partner's inner core. Develop your listening skills and enrich your relationship by incorporating this important habit early.

Pillar 5: Giving up "Tit for Tat"

The temptation to fall into the "what's good for the goose is good for the gander" mentality is apparent in early unions but never dies away by itself. It is simultaneously one of the most seductive and destructive devices a couple can fall back on to punish, manipulate, and escape responsibility. From day 1 of your relationship, avoid this temptation.

Pillar 11: Handling Hot Topics

Although sex and money are of obvious interest to couples living together, the most important part of this pillar is the concluding paragraph: the heart-to-heart connection. For couples living together—whether in new relationships or time-tested ones—remember to keep the heart-to-heart connection between you, that invisible thread between your hearts. Visualizing that precious thread can help keep your troubles in perspective and always less important than your relationship.

Pillar 8: Changing Behaviors, Not Your Partner

This pillar prevents you from breaking your pick on the hard rock of who your partner is—since you can't really change that—and focuses on the far more productive task of changing the *behaviors* you dislike. This posture, which calls for honest self-disclosure rather than blame and manipulation, increases the likelihood of getting your needs met without the hard feelings usually involved in a confrontation. This is an important tool for taking good care of your relationship.

Pillar 12: Resolving Conflicts and Disagreements

This is a most important chapter for marriageless marriages, where disregarded or badly resolved conflicts are especially dangerous to the health and longevity of the relationship. Learning to resolve them well so that both of you get your needs met whenever a conflict arises is crucial to the success of your relationship. When you share a mutual commitment to meeting the needs of both persons, your relationship is growing in fertile soil.

Pillar 14: Growing Yourself

In early relationships, it can be all too easy to lose yourself in a common "we." So happy at last to have found someone wonderful, that seems to be all you need! When you come down to reality, Pillar 14 suggests ways of fostering your growth as an ever-evolving individual who is a more centered, more valuable partner than ever before. Who would want to leave a relationship with someone like that?

Pillar 15: Forging a Bond

Without a marriage license to hold you together, cohabiting partners can benefit from the extra glue provided by forging together a strong emotional bond. The stronger the bond, the more confidence and satisfaction your relationship will provide.

In the end, cohabiting couples must find ways to resolve the same issues as their married counterparts. It is up to you to define what you want together and to make it work for you. A relationship is and always will be what the two of you make it. The basic tools are your love and caring, supported by the three conditions that foster growth and the 16 Pillars of a world class marriage.

(18)

GAY/LESBIAN RELATIONSHIPS

There's this illusion that homosexuals have sex and heterosexuals fall in love. That's completely untrue. Everybody wants to be loved.

—Boy George

The three conditions that promote growth and the 16 Pillars are as applicable to homosexual relationships as they are to heterosexual ones. The quality of the relationship is what matters, not the sexual orientation of its partners. The feedback we have received from an admittedly small number of homosexual couples validates our belief. However, we humbly acknowledge that we make these observations from the outside looking in.

Our perception is that the major distinction between a homosexual relationship and a heterosexual one is the level of social acceptance that the couples are likely to experience. Although homosexual relationships are well accepted in some parts of the world and in some social circles, gay and lesbian couples are generally less accepted. This discrimination can be an additional source of difficulty and stress for the individuals and the relationship, which straight couples don't face.

Pete and Rich have lived together for a year. Pete's family has not been told that they are a couple. Rich has been described as Pete's "roommate" without ever implying that they are sexually and emotionally involved. Now that Pete has accepted a job offer in another city and Rich plans to move with him, they face the task of revealing the true nature of their relationship.

Abby and Carol have lived together for twenty years. Abby is a physician who sees a lot of gays and lesbians in her medical practice. Carol is a psychologist who volunteers her time as an activist for the gay-lesbian center. They are "out" as a lesbian couple and have received the full acceptance of their families and friends. However, almost all of their friends and acquaintances are gay or lesbian, and they feel that their sexual orientation and social activism somewhat isolates them from society at large.

Like heterosexual relationships, gay and lesbian partnerships can be powerful commitments that are central to the lives of the couple, or they can be temporary solutions to loneliness, filled with unrealized hopes. The relationships can be filled with caring and shared goals, or they can be new relationships filled with the excitement and naïveté of the honeymoon. They can be sources of satisfaction or sources of frustration. They reflect the varied personalities and interpersonal skills of the people involved.

IMPACT OF SOCIAL MARGINALIZATION

For many gays and lesbians, society's response to their sexual orientation makes it feel necessary to live a lie with their family and friends, and this pretense can become even more onerous when they move toward a live-in relationship. Like any lie, this one generates an alienation from others and an even more painful alienation from their true selves. This is not only painful but terribly regrettable.

Because we know from research literature that acceptance is an essential ingredient in helping an individual develop as a person, social marginalization represents a profound loss for those gays and lesbians who live without acceptance of their sexual orientation or without the ability to share this facet of their life with family and friends. Anyone denied such acceptance lives in a colder world—one that supplies less-than-optimal emotional food, water, and sunshine. This is a regrettable reality for many gay and lesbian couples.

For others, society's impact on their relationship is even more tangible. Because homosexual unions are in many places denied legal status, this can mean the concomitant denial of health care benefits, inheritance rights, visas for which heterosexual partners are eligible, and other forms of social injustice, including the ability to marry and otherwise be fully recognized as a couple. It is as if society believes that denying these rights and privileges will somehow change their sexual orientation. This is insensitive to their needs as human beings and certainly doesn't persuade anyone to turn straight. Nevertheless, in many circumstances throughout the world, gay and lesbian couples live in societies that cast them in a negative light and deny them full acceptance.

There is, however, a developing trend toward greater social acceptance of homosexual couples, a trend more prevalent in Europe than in the United States. But even in the United States, gays and lesbians are now protected from discrimination in the workplace, and several states have passed legislation supporting gay marriage. As similar legislation is adopted in other states, gay couples will be granted the same important legal rights as those routinely enjoyed by married couples. So while the search for legal equality is incomplete in the United States, there are signs of progress.

However, living in a hostile environment may produce an unexpected advantage. Because gay and lesbian partnerships offer the same emotional meaning as heterosexual unions but exist within a society that generally offers less emotional and legal support, it can be argued that the sanctuary that those relationships represent for the individuals involved is especially cherished and sacred, thus contributing unusual strength to the union and to their sense of being bonded. Although most gay and lesbian couples would probably be willing to trade such a dubious "benefit" for fuller acceptance by society, perhaps it is the proverbial silver lining within the storm clouds of social marginalization.

Jim and John fell in love and after living together for a while decided to have a symbolic wedding ceremony to formalize their commitment to each other. Although gay marriages are not recognized in the state where they live, their ceremony was attended by family and friends, and it was a beautiful event in their lives. They exchanged wedding rings they have now worn for more than twenty years. Their partnership is stronger and more vibrant than those of many of their heterosexual friends.

FINDING A PARTNER

Because homosexuality is not fully accepted throughout society, the first step in finding a partner is an internal process—of accepting that your sexual orientation is not what society, or perhaps even you, expected it to be. For some people, this acceptance comes easily. For others, it represents a struggle played out over many years, accompanied by confusion and pain. Some have the advantage of clarity and social support; others lack these factors. Only when this is resolved within yourself can you embark upon the process of finding a true partner.

> Bill and Margo lived together for fourteen years. He loved her very much but never felt right about marrying, although this was something she had hoped for. After Margo left him for another man, Bill experimented with gay lovers. After several years, he came to see and accept himself as homosexual. Soon thereafter he met Rob, and they quickly formed a strong emotional bond. Rob moved into Bill's home and took a new job so they could be together. Bill has never been happier, "It's so wonderful to go to bed every night and wake up each morning with someone you love and who you know feels the same way about you."

A unique problem homosexuals face is that there is a smaller pool of potential mates, and unlike racial or ethnic minorities, gays and lesbians must find partners from within their minority population. This is further complicated by the fact that some gays and lesbians are "out"—visible in society as homosexuals—while others protect their social and professional standings by remaining socially hidden; some even marry heterosexuals to hide their sexual identity. Though the closeted homosexuals may be visible within the underground gay community, this secrecy can further complicate and limit the search for a suitable partner. As a result, gays and lesbians may be more pessimistic about their chances of finding what they are looking for in a partner and may fear that they will have to make severe compromises in order to have any kind of relationship. Since everyone wants to find his or her dream partner, such thoughts are discouraging. The search for a partner is made even more difficult by the fact that the great majority of dating and mate-finding services focus on heterosexual singles. Traditionally, there have been fewer resources available to gays to assist in finding and establishing satisfying relationships, although the Internet now has narrowed this gap.

EMOTIONAL COMMITMENT

Although levels of emotional commitment in many gay and lesbian unions is indistinguishable from those found in the closest of straight marriages, the unique role of the sexual relationship—the precise factor that sets them apart—can differ for homosexuals.

For many homosexual relationships, the sexual connection is a more important component of the relationship than the emotional one. For these couples, having readily available, compatible, and enjoyable sex is the principal reason for being together. While this is not so different from many young heterosexuals during the sexual excitement of the honeymoon phase, some gay couples are content to keep sex as the centerpiece of their relationship without trying to add much emotional closeness. Perhaps they view the many examples in the straight community of couples who proclaim their deep love yet eventually divorce as a poor and unattractive model to follow.

For many solid, fully committed, and enduring gay relationships, sexual fidelity is not the paramount issue it is for most heterosexual couples. For them, there is a certain tolerance for their partner's sexual encounters with others, and they do not view this as a threat to the relationship in the same way that heterosexual couples often do. For these couples, both parties have emotional permission to have occasional sex with other partners, without resentment or concern.

All of these factors—limited role models, limited pool of choices, and the role of sex in the relationship—may make it more difficult for gays to achieve a deeply satisfying emotional connection. If you are part of a gay or lesbian couple dealing with the typical problems found in a relationship in addition to the added stresses of being part of an oppressed

minority, we urge you to put special emphasis on developing your relationship skills together. This will enable you to increase the likelihood
of creating long-term happiness with your partner and the kind of relationship that helps you deal with discrimination and the other unique
challenges of your relationship. If that is your desire, much of this book
will be helpful, but two chapters in particular—chapter 4, "Using Power
Listening," and chapter 15, "Forging a Bond"—may have special value
for you in the search for your own world class marriage, whether society
allows you to call it that or not.

19

KIDS AND THE RELATIONSHIP

Literature is mostly about having sex and not much about having children. Life is the other way around.

—David Lodge

The arrival of the first child makes an astonishing impact on the new parents' relationship. Nothing that has come before prepares the couple for the change in dynamics that occurs, not even the long months of the pregnancy, because then they are still essentially a twosome.

As soon as the cherished baby arrives, the primary focus of the new parents' lives switches in a flash from pleasing and enjoying each other as lovers and friends to becoming responsible caregivers to an exciting, demanding, and initially helpless new human being. Although children slowly grow less dependent, their needs continue to absorb more of their parents' attention than the parents may have to give to each other for nearly two decades. In short, barring divorce or death, having children disrupts your relationship with each other more than any other event.

THE STRESSES

The parents we surveyed regarding the effects of children on marriage were in remarkable agreement about many negative consequences. And they greeted the opportunity to share their experiences on the subject with surprising relish: "You want to know how kids affect a marriage? Let me tell you!" The effects they were most eager to share are shown in the box below.

KEY WAYS CHILDREN IMPACT A COUPLE'S RELATIONSHIP

- Less time together
- Lack of time, privacy, or drive for sex
- Disagreements over childrearing practices and expectations
- Exhaustion
- Little opportunity or energy for relaxing "dates" together
- Frustration about unequal responsibilities of parenting partners
- Feelings of resentment over these and other problems

Charles, who works at home, and Marie, a full-time mother, have two energetic boys, ages four and seven, and a strong, loving marriage. They describe some of the problems they experience:

"No sex. Too tired for sex. And our moods are so altered by the needs and wants of the children that by the time we talk to each other, we're just mad. . . . Not at each other, but it flows out!"

"There's constant tension, a sort of siege mentality—what's getting broken? Fighting. Bottomless needs. The ongoing grind of bottomless needs. The carryover 24/7."

"There's no time for yourself. Any time left over goes to your partner, but there is no time left over."

"We're in it for the long haul, knowing there will be little ease-up. Becoming a parent is a life-altering decision. . . . They need constant attention. It's the end of selfish endeavors like vacations."

There's a flip side to Charles and Marie's experience, which we will return to. But the question remains: why is the enormity of the impact of children on their parents' lives and relationship so ignored or glossed over by parents, the media, and society? We suspect there are two reasons. First, having children is a simple necessity for carrying on the species, so keeping it attractive has strong, instinctive survival value. No one wants to put down motherhood. Second, the reduced romance, energy, and freedom of the partners are offset by new satisfactions centered around their efforts to do a good job by magically turning this raw material into a fully-functioning, successful new person.

THE JOYS

Although having children can be a major disruption, it also brings unique joys and rewards. Unlike the unanimity regarding the major negative impacts, we received a surprisingly diverse range of positive effects on the relationship. A sample of these responses is listed in the following box.

KEY WAYS CHILDREN POSITIVELY IMPACT THE COUPLE'S RELATIONSHIP

- We're enjoying the rewards of watching our children succeed and achieve.
- We've found a common goal of raising good kids.
- They keep us young and active.
- We have a strong sense of accomplishment from something we achieved.
- Having children broadened our focus from individuals to the whole family.
- Children give us a future to look forward to.

- We feel fulfilled to have made a family.
- We feel challenged to be responsible and humanistic.
- Our two boys helped heal our broken hearts after the loss of our first two children.
- Kids give us a perspective on a hectic world.
- We delight in the joy we see the other get from the kids.
- We are never bored!
- Kids remind us not to argue or shout at each other.
- Our children brought us closer by forcing us to work together to find ways to get through the teen years.
- The love from the kids raised our self-esteem and happiness, so we are happier people and happier in our marriage.
- A greater appreciation of our partner's strengths and skills.

Four of the respondent couples' stories speak eloquently of the rewards children brought to their relationship. Lindsay and Will have a preschool girl who has brought these gifts to them:

> "We share something wonderful—our child! So we share great love, joy, and pride in her. This feeling of shared joy makes us feel more connected and more invested in each other. Some people don't want to hear about all the adorable little things she does—but Will always wants to hear!

> "My parents were divorced, so I find myself wanting to work harder on my relationship with Will to keep it healthy and strong for her so that we can provide her a happy family. It's like an extra reason to invest in my marriage."

Here's how professionals Stephen and Jeanette, whose twelve-year-old son arrived in their early middle age, describe the positive impact he has made on their marriage:

> "Having Blair has given us something to talk about besides architecture and city planning. He keeps us young—we do things we would never do without a child. He stimulates us intellectually and physically. He makes us laugh. He makes us do things together as a family. If we didn't have him around, all we would do is work. We try new things—Jeanette now

likes baseball!—we meet new people, we discuss different issues, we go to ball games, we learned about the Internet, we enjoy the dog we got for him. And when stormy times have hit, the fact that we together have taken on a responsibility for his welfare has kept us married!"

Charles and Marie, whose trials with their two rambunctious boys were described earlier, also reap rewards from parenthood:

"Having these boys has given us a huge sense of completeness that we didn't have when we were just a married couple. And we have the feeling of being complete members of society—school, sports, doctors, meetings, car pooling, birthday parties, and all.

"Our love and pride over their accomplishments (soccer games, art work, etc.) is a wonderful bonus. And their expressions of their love for us are deeply moving, their innocence, their genuine feelings of caring.

"And when we do get away, we're friends and lovers again. The tension drains away and our love for each other is instantly rekindled. So we really have it all."

Janet and Harvey, whose two daughters are twenty and twenty-two, sum up well the positive effects parenthood has had on their marriage:

"We see an interesting seesaw in raising kids. To do it well, you have to put in the time and energy, which in turn puts pressure on the marriage. But if you make that sacrifice, there really is a payoff. Not only for the kids but in the satisfaction derived from the teamwork of the marriage. And certainly one of our biggest goals from the beginning was to raise a family."

Not surprisingly, we concluded that that while couples generally agree that the joys and satisfactions of having children outweigh the stresses and strains, the latter points to a serious need for additional ways to nurture a couple's closeness.

APPLYING THE PILLARS

What steps can you take in the face of this challenge? Here's how some specific pillars of a world class marriage can help.

Pillar 1: Setting Goals

It is best for all concerned if the decision to have a child is made by both partners and is from the outset of the relationship a shared goal. In many instances, however, children arrive when they do, and parenting plans develop thereafter. In either case, focus on making childrearing a shared goal, something that both partners participate in together. In addition to this, review and expand your agreed-upon goals. As a person torn by the competing demands of your child, spouse, and work, you need to be supported in some activity that is truly important to you as an individual more than ever. Enlist the support of your partner and any older children you may have, and do not give it up!

Pillar 2: Avoiding Blame

Be especially aware of the temptation to blame your spouse, your children, your job. The constant stresses of being responsible for infants and growing children tend to make tempers short, and blaming can become an easy palliative. Make a continual effort to remember that everyone—spouse, child, whomever—is doing the best he or she can under the circumstances. That includes you. Remember to own your frustrations and fatigue, and express those feelings in I-Language rather than dumping your frustrations on your partner or child with heaps of blame. As Marie said to us, "I never blame. If I ever started blaming Charles in the middle of all this, I think it would be the beginning of the end!"

Pillar 6: Assuming Self-Responsibility

Assuming self-responsibility is more important than ever when you become a parent. You must see that you get your own needs met. To meet the needs of your family—your spouse and your children—your cup must be as full as possible! If your cup is empty or nearly so, what have you left to give to your loved ones? Endless sacrifice is the most harmful path you can follow, for it leads to your own depletion—the empty cup. Do whatever it takes to achieve a balance between caring for your children and caring for yourself and your partner. Let your resentment be your guide. If you are feeling resentful, it means you are failing to take care of yourself. Call a family meeting, call a babysitter, call your mother, call a counselor—do whatever it takes to refill your cup!

Pillar 4: Using Power Listening

Using power listening may be the most important pillar of all for harried parents. When one of you is down from the stresses and hard work of raising a child, being able to spill your frustrations and upsets to an empathic, accepting spouse who allows you to be as frustrated and upset as you are, can be incredibly healing. Never underestimate the power of being able to express yourself fully without being told to change, or get better, or get a grip. Your ability to give such a gift to each other at times of stress is worth its weight in gold.

Pillar 8: Changing Behaviors, Not Your Partner

The precepts in this pillar are especially helpful, because one of the most common sources of friction with your partner can be disagreement about childrearing. It is more beneficial to confront over a specific parenting action rather than a trend, to express your fears rather than your theories, and to reveal yourself rather than making your partner wrong. Expect your partner to be defensive, but try to grasp the humanity behind his or her actions and defense, and recognize that she or he is always doing his or her best. After nonjudgmental confrontation, your partner may or may not change, but your relationship will still be intact, as will be the rights of both of you as separate parents as well as partners.

Pillar 14: Growing Yourself

Growing yourself is an especially important pillar for stay-at-home, full-time mothers. Your job is so depleting and potentially all consuming that it can be hard even to contemplate continuing to develop yourself as a human being. But again, enlightened selfishness is the path to follow. Do whatever it takes to continue your intellectual, emotional, and spiritual growth by tenaciously planning for time to pursue your growth, utilizing such readily available resources as books, tapes, community college extension classes, television classes, hobby groups, community volunteer work, and online learning. The rewards are great: the excitement of learning, of becoming a more interesting person to your spouse, of having more to give to your family, and of being a more inspiring model to your children, pointing them toward education and growth rather than sacrifice and stagnation.

Pillar 16: Nurturing the Honeymoon

Nurturing the honeymoon tends to get lost in the hubbub of childrearing, but intentionality is more important than time. A quick illustration that serves as a metaphor for many couples: we often see families at the movies seated mother/child/child/father. You and your spouse can hold hands more easily if you're the two in the middle. Don't let the romance die.

Pillar 15: Forging a Bond

If you follow the spirit of the 16 Pillars of a world class marriage to minimize the negative effects of childrearing and maximize its satisfactions and joys, the evidence suggests that becoming parents can be one of the most potent baptisms of fire in forging a strong and lasting bond between you. The intact couples we interviewed whose children were grown spoke of their relationship as having weathered a long but satisfying storm to reach a closer and more mature relationship than before.

To sum up, the impact of children on the marital relationship is vast. Although the satisfactions usually outweigh the difficulties, we urge couples to recognize the major stress involved and take positive steps to protect their closeness. John and Julie Gottman's book, *And Baby Makes Three*, is a valuable reference for learning how to deal with the impact of bringing children into the relationship (see bibliography). Other steps should include learning improved parenting techniques using resources such as Thomas Gordon's *P.E.T.: Parent Effectiveness Training* and remembering to use the applicable world class marriage pillars.

⓴

GETTING MEN TO COMMUNICATE

Man is not the enemy here, but the fellow victim.

—Betty Friedan

Although the title of this chapter resonates with many people, both men and women, some male readers may be offended by it, feeling it implies that men are innately less willing or less able to communicate than women. They may feel we discriminate against the male of the species by viewing them as defective in this regard and requiring expert intervention to measure up to women's superior abilities. Let's clarify.

First of all, there are far greater differences between men and women than their ability to express ideas and understand what is heard. We know of no innate differences between men and women's abilities to communicate. However, a study using functional magnetic resonance imaging (fMRI) conducted by the Indiana University School of Medicine revealed that the way men and women listen is structurally different. As they listened to a novel read to them, a majority of the men in the study showed exclusive activity in the temporal lobe in the left side of the brain, whereas the women showed a left temporal dominance but also showed activity in the right temporal lobe as well. Radiologist Dr. Michael Phillips, coauthor of the study, notes that their interest is in figuring out what normal is and "more and more often it seems that normal for men may be different than normal for women. That doesn't mean that one is better than the other." Co-researcher Dr. Joseph T. Lurito adds, "we don't know if the difference is because of the way we're raised or if it's hardwired in the brain. We will never be able to figure that out completely."[10]

In human interaction, differences generally arise in communicating and understanding emotions and feelings. In many relationships, neither partner has a problem communicating in this arena. In others, it is the woman who is more emotionally tongue-tied. But whether it's from biological differences or the way that boys are socialized in many cultures, the man is often the partner who has more difficulty in relationships where this is an issue.

Because this is a source of much pain and frustration for these men and for their partners, we believe it warrants special attention. We hope the reader can relate to what we see as an important human problem experienced to a large extent but certainly not exclusively by men.

THE SOCIALIZATION OF MEN

It's a cruel game we play with our boys. We say to them: "Be brave." "Don't cry." "Take it like a man." We teach our boys to ignore, to minimize, to disregard, and to overcome feelings of weakness. We teach them to be strong and not flinch in the face of danger. We teach them not to have "unmanly" feelings.

Then, twenty-five years later, we marry one of them and we say to him: "Talk to me." "Tell me your feelings." "I want to be close to you." We wonder why it's hard for this lovely man to open up and share his feelings with the person he most loves. We complain that he "doesn't know a feeling from a barn door." Small wonder!

Most men are not rewarded as children for being sensitive and for sharing their feelings. They are bred for bravery, as it were, not for being in touch with their feelings, but for denying this part of themselves. Moreover, adult men continue to be reinforced for being strong and capable, for keeping a steady hand on the tiller, for being able to "overcome their feelings." This is the culture of the workplace where men thrive. As Warren Farrell puts it in *Women Can't Hear What Men Don't*

Say (see bibliography), a man receives his pay by becoming a "human doing," not a human being.

To compound matters, many women still look to men to take care of them—as "human doings" who retain the Neanderthal ability to be successful killer-protectors. Like women, who often are judged on the basis of their physical beauty as potential partners, men are often considered attractive for their professional accomplishments: the beauty queen and the millionaire. Neither standard does much to encourage the humanity of the people involved.

The societal pressure to be successfully strong is very powerful, and it exerts a subtle, persistent pressure on boys and men to disown certain "troublesome" aspects of their internal experience. The tragedy of this is that when you deny parts of yourself, as millions of boys around the world are taught to do, these parts eventually become unavailable. Anything that is not allowed to be experienced is either denied or repressed. The unfortunate by-product of years of denial and repression is that important emotional components of your self are eventually walled off, making them hard, if not impossible, to access. A man who has always believed it was unacceptable to show his "weaker" side—feelings of fear, aloneness, or uncertainty—eventually won't have any sense of having these feelings. When asked if he's worried or upset about something, he's likely to answer, "Not particularly." He's not lying. He's not minimizing. He simply doesn't feel this feeling. He's been taught in the **socialization** process that those kinds of feelings aren't acceptable to have. Consequently, he has pushed these feelings into internal places so remote that he believes he no longer has these troubling feelings. Nothing seems to bother him. He can even go into battle without showing his fear. This is what we have traditionally asked of our men, and our men learn to do it. To ask this man to "share" is to cause frustration for both of you.

Oh, yes, it may be inside him somewhere, but it will not be easy for him to access it, and it may be impossible, short of intensive therapy.

THE PROBLEMS OF DENIAL

The scenario gets even worse: when human beings use denial as a way to deal with troublesome feelings, this primitive coping mechanism has the unsettling habit of blocking out other feelings as well. Thus, when we deny our feelings of fear, for example, this is likely to cause difficulty in experiencing joy as well. Denial is a nonspecific coping mechanism. Thus, using it with troublesome emotions minimizes a person's capacity to experience pleasant ones. These people have less difficult lows but less wonderful highs—the roller coaster of life has fewer chills and thrills, a much flatter ride.

> Michael and Patricia often go hiking and camping together. Patricia talks excitedly about every adventure—the beauty of the countryside, of the animals, flowers, birds that they see. Michael focuses his attention on making sure that all the camping gear is packed properly and that nothing is forgotten.

> Cassie and Frank have just bought a new home. Cassie is excited about painting and decorating their bedroom. Frank just wants to make sure they have enough money to pay the bills.

> When Nathan's father died, he appeared to be upset but never talked about it. His only comment was, "What can you expect? He had a heart attack."

Men can pay a terrible price for not being allowed access to their full range of emotions as a child. Not to be allowed to feel scared or cry or exhibit other "unmanly" emotions teaches boys to become stoic, unfeeling, unresponsive men. Strong warriors, to be sure, but these strong warriors aren't likely to be able to deliver the emotional intimacy that their wives want.

> Colin works for a difficult boss. Although Colin makes many important contributions, his boss largely ignores them, and his heavy-handed criticisms are often hard to bear. Although he stoically minimizes these feelings at home, his wife, Margit, senses his pain, but she doesn't have the skills to help him fully experience it. Colin, well trained as a "human doing," greets her anguish by justifying his boss's actions and minimizing their effects on him. This distresses Margit even more—she wishes that Colin would recognize how badly he is treated and speak up to his boss about it or change jobs.

Dick and Katherine have been together for four years. Dick seldom expresses his feelings about anything, and it bothers Katherine that he never says he loves her except when he's had a few drinks. Then the feelings come out and Katherine hears how important she is to Dick. She wishes he would say this to her when he hasn't had any liquor.

Warren's an accountant, at home with computers and ledger sheets, but less fluent in the language of feelings. His children make a point of calling attention to it whenever they discover him wiping away a tear after seeing a movie. "Look at Dad! He's crying!" they announce. Warren endures this little humiliation and does his best to remove the traces of momentary weakness and restore his normal composure.

It is obvious from these examples that the "manly-man" complex we instill in our males damages their emotional ability to react in ways that further some of their own best interests. It limits their ability to experience some aspects of life, and it can frustrate the people in their lives who wish to have an intimate, caring relationship with them.

THE COMPLEXITY OF OUR EXPECTATIONS FOR MEN

Part of the problem is that we train boys not to experience their "softer" emotions, and this is further reinforced for them in the workplace as adults. Added to that is the yin and yang of marriage partners who want their men both to be successful "human doings," while at the same time capable of emotional intimacy. The final component of the profound double bind handed to men is an outgrowth of the women's movement, which seems now to demand that men be fully involved in homemaking and childrearing, sensitive to women's needs, and emotionally labile and sexually satisfying, while still being strong and successful in their own careers.

A great deal is asked of today's man, and very little is done to help him succeed at this new paradigm of manhood. Bred to succeed according to the old standards, how are men going to develop the capacity to succeed in this emotionally complex new world?

PROVIDING THE CONDITIONS FOR GROWTH

Society today asks men to grow. How can this be accomplished? The research literature provides a clear perspective on the conditions that create the capacity to grow. They are our old friends, empathy, acceptance, and genuineness. We know that professional therapists who provide these conditions to their clients are successful in supporting the characterological change that helps them develop the capacity to deal more successfully with their problems. Moreover, research evidence clearly shows that these three characteristics are the most important factors in helping clients deal with their problems—more important than any other variable in the counselor-client relationship. Why should any marriage partner offer less to the person he or she loves?

Men, like all human creatures, need empathy and acceptance and thrive best in authentic, congruent relationships. A marriage—or any close emotional partnership—should be founded upon and infused with these three powerful conditions. When these conditions are freely and continually available to both partners in the relationship, both partners can feel emotionally safe. Out of safety comes growth. Out of growth comes the capacity to experience and express deeper emotions. Out of this, emotional intimacy and profound feelings of closeness are created. For men and others with limited emotional lability, this can be the slow-but-steady path away from emotional rigidity and inexpressiveness.

The need for this warm, helpful scenario to be actualized is very widespread. Many relationships start with emotionally unavailable men pairing with women who have rudimentary skills in expressing empathy, acceptance, and genuineness. Unfortunately, the reverse is also common, with emotionally unavailable women pairing with unskilled men.

CREATING CHANGE IN YOUR RELATIONSHIP

How do you develop the capacity to provide these three powerful conditions in your love relationship?

You start with the stated intention to follow this path and an agreement together to work on your capacities to provide these conditions (a shared goal). Then you establish a plan to learn power listening skills (which provides empathy and acceptance) and I-Language (which provide a vehicle for genuineness). You work together to master these skills, recognizing that it will take time and effort to become proficient. You encourage each other to talk and share regularly, so that you each have the chance to practice listening skills, and you encourage each other to confront with I-Messages and to work out conflicts so that both of you get your needs met. You set up a climate of growth, of sharing, of developing together—a safe atmosphere the two of you create that enables you both to become people who can provide the conditions that foster personal and relationship growth.

As part of your work on power listening, focus on becoming aware of and summarizing, or feeding back, your understanding of each other's nonverbal as well as verbal behavior. Pay attention to the subtle cues available—shifts in facial expression, body language, tone of voice. Partners can readily learn to observe and understand each other's nonverbal cues. Long ago, I noticed that Ralph always sniffs when he's mad—I can spot the sniff right before he finds the words to express his anger. When he's really upset, it's two sniffs. Other partners report: "Craig's jaw muscle twitches when he's upset." "Just the way Maria walked into the room, I knew something was wrong." "If he isn't talking, something big is going on."

Gently power listen the nonverbal cues you observe—"Looks like you're upset, Craig"—then perhaps gently offer a door opener: "Do you want to talk about it?" Look serious, interested, and safe to talk to. Intend to be safe to talk to. Intend to listen and do everything necessary to restrain yourself from offering advice or any other comment or question that could in any way divert his conversational direction from where he wants to go. Give your partner a real opportunity to share with you. Do your part to enable this to happen—learn how to use these beneficial skills.

Albert is married to a much younger woman. Although his health has always been excellent, he is afraid his advancing age will bring sickness and debilitation. He doesn't feel he has the right to marry a younger woman and then get sick, and he is afraid that any signs of illness would be profoundly upsetting to his wife. He has lately experienced some chest pains and is afraid to tell his wife about them, so he swallows his concern.

Damon hasn't been happy for the past three years and knows it has to do with his job. He feels he's trapped in a dead-end situation but doesn't know what to do. He doesn't even know what he's looking for and is afraid to consider alternatives because of the impact on his family, for whom he's the primary means of financial support. He's depressed and worried about his future.

If you are the partners of these men, you must be willing to help them down from their pedestals as strong, stoic supermen. Let go of any explicit or implicit demand that they remain human doings. If you want to develop emotional intimacy with this complex and troubled partner—and everyone's partner is troubled sometimes—you must make peace with the fact that this seeming tower of strength also can suffer from fear, weakness, hurt, regret, and sadness. To the extent that you can reconcile yourself to and accept these feelings in your partner, you create safety for him to experience and express these feelings to you. This opens the door to true growth.

Over time, with a shared commitment between the two of you and focused attention on skill building together, wonderful things can happen. Your comfort level and skills develop so that you become a capable listener, and your partner becomes more comfortable sharing his personal concerns. Your partner may become more attuned to his emotions through your use of power listening, linking his nonverbal behaviors with verbal expressions of emotion. Your partner may gain greater access to his emotions from long-term exposure to this safe emotional environment. Your partner may experience the opportunity to become more authentically and more deeply himself.

Do not underestimate the importance of empathically and acceptingly feeding back the nonverbal messages of people who aren't strong verbal communicators. There are two reasons for doing this: (1) Most communication is nonverbal (about 93 percent) with more than 60 percent being nonvocal (no words or tone of voice), so body language and facial expression provide a rich collection of signals not to be overlooked. (2) Everybody communicates all the time. For example, silence itself sends a message that people unconsciously recognize and interpret without actually thinking of it as communication. Silence can mean many things: I'm upset, but afraid to express it. I'm busy with my thoughts, which are important to me. I'm too tired to talk. I feel overwhelmed by everything and don't want to think about it any more. I'm working on something and don't want to be disturbed. If you empathically reflect back to your partner your best guess about what his silence is saying, you will receive feedback regarding your accuracy in decoding the nonverbal message, and you may encourage further verbal communication.

To overlook nonverbal communication and complain, "My husband never talks to me!" is to miss a chance to make it safer for him to express more and an opportunity to increase your sense of closeness together.

EMOTIONALLY SAFE CONFRONTATION

While power listening communicates empathy and acceptance, it is not always possible to provide these supportive conditions, because there are times when you don't feel empathic and accepting. When your partner does things that are upsetting to you or create a problem for you, it becomes necessary to confront, and though many people fear confrontation, it is an opportunity to provide the third supportive condition for growth: genuineness.

As we have discussed, confrontation is best accomplished through the use of an I-Message in which you express to your partner, without blame, how his or her behavior impacts you. The importance of confrontation without blame is underscored by John Gottman and Nan Silver's research (*The Seven Principles for Making Marriage Work*; see the bibliography), which has documented the profound damage done to relationships from confrontations beginning with a "harsh start." Gottman identifies a **harsh start** as any discussion that leads off with criticism or sarcasm, a form of contempt. His research shows that harsh starts are one of the key predictors of divorce and are closely related to others, including defensiveness, "stonewalling," "flooding," and rejected attempts at repairing damage. Harsh starts are the critical beginning of a cascade that can trigger many of the other divorce predictors.

A common scenario goes like this: The wife, who in many relationships is the one who most often identifies a problem, confronts her husband with a harsh, critical start. The husband feels defensive and reacts with elevated blood pressure and hormonal changes including the secretion of adrenaline that kicks in the "fight or flight" response. This is the physiological response known as **flooding**. As a means of handling the flooding—the sense of being overwhelmed—the male withdraws emotionally and refuses to deal with the problem. This is the tactic known as **stonewalling**. The wife responds by complaining further about his emotional withdrawal, perhaps adding some contempt to this combustive mix, further reinforcing her partner's need for emotional isolation, which further exasperates the wife: He's impossible to deal with! She's impossible to deal with! What's the use of even trying! The merry-go-round of marriage becomes decreasingly merry, and the relationship may soon be in serious trouble.

Supporting research by Robert Levenson and Loren Carter at the University of California at Berkeley found that when male subjects are stressed, their hearts actually beat faster than females and remain accelerated for a longer period of time.[11] Dolf Zillman, a psychologist at the University of Alabama, found that when male subjects are treated rudely and then told to relax, their blood pressure surges and stays elevated until they get to retaliate. In contrast, women experiencing similar situations can generally calm down within a period of twenty minutes.[12] These studies both indicate that marital confrontation—especially those characterized by harsh starts—takes a greater physiological toll on the male, setting him up to become temporarily disabled or requiring some kind of retaliation in order to gain emotional release. Therefore, it comes as no surprise that men would wish to avoid difficult confrontations, and it behooves women to avoid harsh starts, if they wish to keep their partners engaged in the discussion and responsive to their concerns.

If this discussion isn't compelling enough, research from Gottman's Love Lab indicates that what most damages the sexual relationship for men is destructive conflict with their wives.[13] Although improving the couple's friendship is generally the most important pathway to sex for women, improving conflict resolution turns out to be the most common pathway to better sex for men. Since harsh starts are the quickest way to derail successful conflict resolution, women who want their partners to be more affectionate should keep this vividly in mind.

Giving up damaging communication patterns such as harsh, blameful confrontation takes real work. Confrontational style becomes a habit just as any other, and habits are notoriously hard to break. Furthermore, under emotional pressure—which characterizes most confrontational situations—we are prone to revert to old habits. Additionally, the process of self-monitoring is tricky; it's easy to think you're not as blameful and critical as your partner may interpret you to be. It helps to remind yourself continually that your intention is not to hurt or blame your partner; your intention is to communicate genuinely about yourself—to reveal yourself in an open and vulnerable way in order to increase the likelihood of getting your needs met.

For the man, it also takes work to stay in the process and not become overwhelmed when confronted. However painful it feels to be flooded, it's a familiar reaction that takes a calm discipline to overcome. If your partner has made a commitment to decreasing the harshness of her confrontation, you must remind yourself of your partner's intent to change and somehow gather the perspicacity to acknowledge that your partner may not be blaming and criticizing you.

MAKING PROGRESS TOGETHER

If a woman wants the benefit of her "uncommunicative" male partner's communication, it is important to (1) resist sending any message that blocks his sharing; (2) become skilled at deciphering and feeding back your partner's verbal and nonverbal messages; and (3) extract harshness, blame, and criticism from your words, tone of voice, and intentions. This requires real honing of your listening and confrontation skills. A spouse eager for more friendship and emotional intimacy must do her part by learning how to provide the conditions that foster her partner's willingness and capacity for more intimate time together. This is not easy for the female nor for the male, but it can be very rewarding for both.

Another interesting way to work on this together is through a process of relaxation and stress reduction. Find some written instructions for doing this, perhaps with the wife reading them to her husband in a soft, soothing voice, while the husband uses visualization to wash his body free of anxiety. In this way, the wife's voice is associated in her husband's mind with soothing and relaxation rather than with harsh starts, criticism, and blame. Over time, this can significantly change the dynamics of the relationship in positive ways. (See Joan Borysenko's *Minding the Body, Mending the Mind* for some practical stress reduction techniques.)

Men are asked to evolve in their capacities for sharing feelings and for engaging in emotionally intimate relationships. For a "human doing" type of man, this can entail a profoundly scary risk: uncovering then acknowledging to himself and to his partner feelings he has been taught since childhood to hide and ignore. To do this, he must take the risk that despite previous experiences, it may—this time, with this loving, caring partner—be safe. This involves looking the tiger in the eye and walking toward it. Reclaiming, owning, sharing, and dealing with long-banished emotions takes courage and the will to overcome many old internal signals.

Yet, men, this is what your partner is asking of you. This is intimacy. This is sharing. This is closeness. And this is the emotional fiber that binds a relationship. Your partner asks this of you, and society now values the man who can be successful at home as well as at work. Yet the manly-man, back-to-the jungle conditioning males receive can be so powerful that it may seem as if they are being asked both to mutate their own genes and resist all previous conditioning. But the jungle and the caveman are no longer appropriate models, and men deserve to experience and be supported for the full range of their emotional lives and to know the intimacy and joy that can bring.

For our men to evolve their capacities to share intimately, their partners must evolve also—into empathic, nonjudgmental listeners and non-blameful, emotionally vulnerable confronters. Women must do their part if they ask their partners to expose their deepest selves. Women must make it safe for men to talk, and that includes *not* demanding that they do so. And both must accept that this is a process that will take time.

Marriage and emotional partnerships are about growth. For some men to become full emotional partners despite our culture's early conditioning, both parties must be willing to develop their potentialities as human beings and to share these with their partner. The amazing and thrilling by-product of this challenge is that it can actually expand your mental capacities. Research studies increasingly show that mental challenge builds brain structure and that enhanced mental capacities are an important hedge against the ravages of aging. Potential benefits to your mental capacity is an additional payoff for the struggle you face in changing old habits and developing new relationship-enhancing ones. This is most certainly a gift that keeps on giving.

Few of us, not just men, are fortunate enough to enter into our love relationship with all the communication skills we need and experience ease and comfort in sharing our deepest feelings. For most of us, these are important areas in which we need to grow. Learning how to provide your partner with a climate wherein growth can occur and taking the risk to share intimately within this climate are essential building blocks of the relationship. Working on this together can produce profound growth, not only for the man, but also for his partner, and for the level of satisfaction you experience in your relationship together.

21

BEING YOURSELF
IN THE RELATIONSHIP

Only the educated are free.

—Epictetus

In this book, we talk a lot about communication skills to use when you or your partner are upset or under stress. We have urged you to learn new listening and talking skills, with the object of improving your ability to help yourself and each other when the emotional chips are down.

Yet as a psychologist friend of ours once said, "Who wants a skilled friend?" The mental image this suggests is of an individual responding mechanically in a clinically "correct" but utterly dehumanized way. This would be a sorry friendship and an even sorrier marriage. Yet excellent internal and external communication are vital in expressing empathy, acceptance, and genuineness, and excellent communication abilities are not naturally acquired by most people in the process of growing up. Unfortunately, most of us do not grow up in an environment where parents showed great empathy and acceptance because, to a great extent, the process of growing up is stressed by the fact that we make thousands of mistakes that our parents work to "correct." The process of correcting our mistakes and teaching us better ways of doing things involves judgment and criticism. It may be done out of a loving desire to see us grow up successfully, but the process is inherently one of criticism, teaching, and many times with our parents telling us the solutions we should use to solve our problems.

Because most of us didn't receive great amounts of empathy and acceptance, we don't have a strong model of this inside us from which to draw. Therefore, as we mature into adults and form friendships and ultimately a marriage relationship, the only ways we know to "help" our friends and our marital partner when they have problems is the model we learned from our parents: judgment, criticism, and advice, all extended with the best of intentions. Unfortunately, experience shows that judgment, criticism, and advice do not facilitate the capacity of people to grow in their ability to deal with their problems. So we are faced with learning how to replace them with empathy and acceptance.

We must also learn to be congruent—honest, authentic, real. Unfortunately, our early experiences teach us that saying what we feel gets us into all kinds of trouble—despite the fact that we're simultaneously being told that honesty is the best policy. We learn to cover up mistakes to avoid punishment, to pretend to have nice feelings to avoid lectures on how to behave, and to play certain roles to get taken seriously. These incidental but powerful experiences often leave our congruence in tatters, and we go through life playing the part that we have learned avoids trouble the most efficiently. But our partner can grow best if she or he can trust that we are who we present ourselves to be—empathic, accepting, genuine. Therefore, when we power listen, we must ensure that we genuinely care and are genuinely accepting. When we confront through a self-revealing I-Message, we must ensure that message is real and not contrived to play the role. Our mate must see the real us.

Having to learn these new ways of relating as adults causes another, although temporary, problem. Since they are new to us, most of us will find them cumbersome and unfamiliar while we are learning how to implement them. Beneficial as they will become, our initial awkwardness raises the specter of sounding like one of those phony therapist caricatures parodied in the movies—stiff, wooden, and utterly unattractive as a human being: "Ummmm, I hear that you have a problem."

Does it have to be that way? Certainly not. But starting to learn these skills on your way to finding your own natural ability to be congruent, empathic, and accepting will certainly feel awkward. This is partly because the world around you is still stuck in the almost universal mode of judging, criticizing, and advising whenever problems occur, making your new approach feel foreign or unnatural, and partly because learning new skills is inherently awkward, be it interpersonal skills or a new pastime. As this is a well-known phenomenon across skill development in many areas of life, we developed a four-phase description of this type of learning curve:

Phase 1: Ignorance—You don't have the skills and you aren't aware that you don't have any. This is the "ignorance is bliss" stage. Having read this far in the book already, you are no longer in phase one.

Phase 2: Awareness and Guilt—You have learned what the skills are and realize that you haven't been using them when appropriate. You feel bad about the way you "naturally" respond when problems arise and wish that you could handle them differently.

Phase 3: Awkwardness—You have started to learn the skills and are working on developing your technique. You are quite aware of the difficulties involved. At this stage, you may be able to respond correctly at times, but you are still awkward and worry that you sound strange to others, although you are beginning to achieve success. You wonder how long this awkward period will last.

Phase 4: Full Integration of Skills and Personality—If you continue practicing the skills at every opportunity, you will at last reach this stage. This is freedom! This is happiness! You use skills when appropriate, and it is done automatically and naturally—without having to think about it or remind yourself how to do it. This is the point at which the skills are fully integrated into your personality and no longer sound or feel like skills. Yet you have greatly increased your capacity to deal with problem situations successfully.

Knowing what to expect as you move through the four stages will save you from discouragement, but the trip from ignorance to integration involves work and time and, like any skill development, is not easy. To handle the early awkwardness with your partner, acknowledge it right away and agree to cut each other generous amounts of slack as you each do your best to learn the new ways. For the other key people in your life, we recommend that you make the process easier for yourself by telling them that you are undergoing this process of change and ask them to support you.

Beyond that, we encourage you and your mate to keep clearly in mind the real purpose behind learning communication skills and following the 16 Pillars in this book—getting in touch with each other's humanity. This means:

- Moving beyond techniques and skills to finding how alike the two of you are in your needs, feelings, hopes, and fears, and being able to connect with each other in deep and satisfying ways;
- Learning that underneath all the petty disagreements and annoyances of life your fondest hope and desire is to support and care for each other with all of your tenderness and strength;
- And discovering—despite all your superficial flaws and blemishes—what magnificent human beings both you and your partner truly are.

What you are looking for is not mechanical technique or even mechanical mastery. Following the skills and pillars in this book is a path toward rediscovering your own innate, natural ability to connect fully with your shared humanity as two loving human beings. That is the true goal of a world class marriage.

CONCLUDING THOUGHTS

A world class marriage is a dynamic relationship, always growing and evolving and always grounded in trust, caring, sensitivity, and skills. We have presented sixteen essential pillars that will help make your marriage world class. We know from our own more than thirty-year relationship how profoundly rewarding this can be. It can be for you and your loving partner, too.

In closing, let us remind you of the fundamentals:

- give the gifts of empathy, acceptance, and genuineness—the three ingredients that most contribute to personal growth;
- commit to finding solutions that meet both partners' needs;
- take responsibility for getting your needs met in life and for developing yourself as a person;
- learn how to communicate your caring in ways that resonate for your partner and be generous in so doing;
- surrender, apologize, and forgive when appropriate;
- nurture the honeymoon feelings;
- and finally, keep the heart-to-heart connection strong at all times.

These fundamentals take practice, and they take commitment. A full complement of these skills is rarely picked up naturally from childhood, and they aren't included with a marriage certificate. Most people have to work hard to recognize and then undo the less-than-helpful patterns they bring into the relationship with their partner.

When you spot your undesirable behaviors, remember not to blame yourself (it doesn't help). Instead, give yourself kind but genuine acceptance (that does help), and simply observe the old pattern playing itself out ("That's me!"). Then go back and clean it up with your partner by using your new fundamentals. Using this method, your undesirable patterns gradually weaken and fade away as you replace them with the skills learned from this book. This can be a difficult, even exasperating, process, but one that delivers many rewards.

In the end, creating a world class marriage is like life itself. It's not the end result that is to be savored so much as the process. And the process of creating a world class marriage is one of sharing, intimacy, and joy. It is a long pathway that you share together with wondrous treasures hidden all along the way.

We are confident that the insights in this book will greatly benefit your relationship, and we extend you our very best wishes for enjoying a long and satisfying world class marriage.

NOTES

1. Benjamin Scafidi, "The Taxpayer Costs of Divorce and Unwed Childbearing" (New York: Institute for American Values, 2008).

2. Diane Sollee, Coalition for Marriage, Family, and Couples Education, www.smartmarriages.com.

3. John M. Gottman and Nan Silver, *The Seven Principles for Making Marriage Work* (New York: Crown Publishers, 1999).

4. C. B. Truax, "Effective Ingredients in Psychotherapy: An Approach to Unraveling the Patient-Therapist Interaction," *Journal of Counseling Psychology* 10 (1963): 256–63; also Robert R. Carkhuff and Bernard G. Berenson, *Beyond Counseling and Therapy* (New York: Holt, Rinehart and Winston, Inc., 1967).

5. Philip Blumstein and Pepper Schwartz, *American Couples: Money, Work, Sex* (New York: Morrow, 1983).

6. For more information, see Dr. Gordon's books *P.E.T: Parent Effectiveness Training* (New York: New American Library, 1970) and *L.E.T.: Leader Effectiveness Training: The No-Lose Way to Release the Productive Potential in People* (New York: Bantam, 1980).

7. John Gottman, *Why Marriages Succeed or Fail . . . and How You Can Make Yours Last* (New York: Fireside, 1994), p. 181.

8. J. R. Gibb, "Defense Level and Influence Potential in Small Groups," in *Leadership and Interpersonal Behavior*, edited by L. Petrullo and B. M. Bass (New York: Holt, Rinehart and Winston, 1961), pp. 66–81.

9. David Popenoe and Barbara Defoe Whitehead, "The State of Our Unions: The Social Health of Marriage in America" (Princeton, NJ: The National Marriage Project, 2002), http://marriage.rutgers.edu.

10. M. Phillips and J. T. Lurito, "Men Do Hear—But Differently than Women, Brain Images Show," press release, 28 November 2002, http://www.medicine.indiana.edu/news_releases/archive_00/men_hearing00.html.

11. John M. Gottman and Nan Silver, *The Seven Principles for Making Marriage Work* (1999). (New York: Random House, 1999), p. 37.

12. John M. Gottman and Nan Silver, *The Seven Principles for Making Marriage Work* (1999). (New York: Random House, 1999), p. 37.

13. Gottman Institute, 2002, www.gottman.com.

GLOSSARY

acceptance: Feeling comfortable with your partner the way he or she is; having no need or desire to change him or her. Acceptance of your partner's thoughts and feelings is one of the three most powerful ways you can help him or her deal with a problem. Acceptance is conveyed through power listening.

active listening: Showing empathy to your partner by summarizing your partner's thoughts and feelings. *See* power listening.

agreed-upon goal: A goal of one person that is supported by his or her partner.

aliveness: Being full of energy and vigor; having a zest for and interest in life.

anticommitment defenses: Thoughts or means you have of leaving the relationship. Giving up anticommitment defenses is a sign of high-level commitment to the relationship.

apology: A statement of remorse about having done something that hurt your partner or an admission of wrongdoing. Effective apologies come from genuine remorse about your hurtful behavior and do not include any justification about why you did what you did.

authenticity: Genuineness; making your words and body language accurately reflect your inner thoughts and feelings. Research by Carl

Rogers indicates authenticity is one of the three most powerful ways to help someone grow.

behavior: Something that a person says or does. Behavior is tangible—something you can see, hear, or touch. When confronting another person, it is important to confront about his or her behavior, not your interpretations or judgments about the behavior or the other person's motivations, character, or intent.

bid for attention: Any attempt to get your partner's attention. Gottman's research data show that high levels of failed bids for attention are a predictor of divorce.

blame: The act of attributing fault for something that has happened. Because blame is likely to trigger defensiveness and reduce cooperation, confronting with blame is usually unsuccessful.

bonding: The process of binding yourself together as a couple, of forming a close emotional tie that cannot be broken.

coerced reciprocation: Saying or doing something for which your partner feels obligated to repay you in some way.

conflict: A serious disagreement between you and your partner that the confrontation cycle fails to resolve, usually involving something one person does that causes a problem for the other. Because conflicts occur in all relationships and unsuccessful conflict resolution results in the erosion of relationship satisfaction, it is important for couples to learn and use skills that help them find mutually satisfying solutions to their conflicts. *See* confrontation cycle.

conflict of needs: A common misunderstanding that one person's needs can be in conflict with another's. Every person has needs, and everyone has the right to try to get those needs met. The needs are not in conflict, it is the means by which individuals attempt to satisfy those needs that are in conflict. Conflicts are more properly understood as a "conflict of solutions," wherein one partner's solution to his or her needs conflicts with the needs of his or her partner.

confrontation cycle: The process for successful confrontation, consisting of sending your partner an XYZ message followed by power listening, which enables your partner to feel heard and understood. This enables him or her to be able to hear and respond caringly to the distress your XYZ message expresses. The typical confrontation cycle consists of four steps:

Step 1: XYZ message.

Step 2: Power listening to your partner's potentially defensive response until your partner feels heard and understood, and he or she is no longer defensive.

Step 3: Repeating your XYZ message or a modified version of it.

Step 4: Continuing steps 2 and 3 until your partner indicates a willingness to find a solution that will solve this problem for you.

See XYZ message.

contempt: An act of dislike and disrespect toward your partner (e.g., eye rolling). Any behavior that conveys that your partner is not worthy of respect. One of Gottman's seven predictors of divorce.

"cool" talk: Popular, trendy, or ironic forms of communication that are often ambiguous in meaning and increase the likelihood for misunderstanding and for causing pain when used in an intimate relationship. Can be fun in small doses, but risky.

criticism: A negative judgment about your partner that indicates disapproval, especially concerning your partner's character, judgment, or worthiness. One of Gottman's seven predictors of divorce.

defensive climates: Behaviors or attitudes that create an environment in which it is likely that your partner will feel criticized or unsafe and feel the need to defend his or her behavior.

defensiveness: An attempt to deflect or avoid blame or criticism. Defensiveness often occurs during a confrontation, especially when the confrontation is blameful. One of Gottman's seven predictors of divorce.

denial: A psychological process by which someone is unwilling or unable to acknowledge a particular behavior, condition, or situation that has negative implications.

empathic listening. *See* power listening.

empathy: Putting yourself in your partner's shoes in an attempt to understand his or her thoughts and feelings. Empathy is best expressed by repeating the gist of your partner's troubled message to him or her, a skill we call power listening. It is the most powerful thing you can do to help your partner deal with a problem. This skill is also referred to as power listening, reflective listening, and active listening.

failed repair attempt: An attempt to restore closeness or lighten the tension during a conflict by the use of humor or by some other means that is rejected by your partner. Failed repair attempts are one of Gottman's seven predictors of divorce.

flooding: A physiological state characterized by increased heart rate and blood pressure, an adrenaline surge, and a sense of being overwhelmed; a likely response to repeated verbal attacks. One of Gottman's seven predictors of divorce.

forgiveness: Being willing to pardon your partner for having done something that was hurtful to you. True forgiveness must include abstaining from any form of punishment for your partner's hurtful behavior.

gist: The main point or essential meaning of something. The means for showing empathy for your partner is by power listening the gist of his or her message to you.

growing yourself: One of the primary means by which you can increase your skills as a human being and increase your satisfaction with your own life.

harsh start: Starting a confrontation harshly, such as with blame, criticism, shouting, or any behavior that is likely to hurt your partner's feelings and cause defensiveness. Gottman's research shows that disagreements begun with a harsh start almost never resolve themselves amicably. He identifies harsh starts as one of the seven predictors of divorce.

heart-shaped words: Expressions that communicate your love, appreciation, and commitment to your partner.

heart-to-heart connection: The notion that the two of you as partners are connected through an invisible bond that connects your hearts. Whatever you say or do, you must not break this connection.

hot topic: A subject with unusually high emotional meaning (e.g., sex, politics, religion, in-laws, money) that requires recognition of the high emotional stakes involved and the need for using the skills that provide maximum empathy, genuineness, and acceptance.

I-Message: The most effective way to confront your partner about a behavior that is unacceptable to you. It consists of three parts:

1. A nonblameful description of the behavior that is a problem for you.
2. The effects of that behavior on you.
3. Your feelings about those effects.

The strength of an I-Message is its self-revealing nature: it describes you, not your partner. This is also called an XYZ message.

in-it-together behaviors: Things you do or say that increase the sense of being connected as a couple.

intention: The quality of purposefulness in regard to accomplishing a goal. Having the intention to succeed in the relationship with your partner is a powerful ingredient in creating that success.

interpretation: An explanation you create in your own mind about the meaning or significance of your partner's behavior. This creates resistance when used in a confrontation.

love language: The means by which you or your partner most readily experience the sense of being loved. Gary Chapman identified five common love languages and found that each person has one or two that has the most meaning for them.

marriage education: Classes for couples that teach research-based skills of effective communication and conflict resolution that enhance closeness, caring, cooperation, and satisfaction between partners.

nonverbal blame: A blameful message that is communicated not in words but by tone of voice, gestures, or other forms of body language.

nonverbal communication: Communication through various forms of body language, including gestures and tone of voice. It is estimated that 93 percent of communication is nonverbal. Because it is not validated with words, nonverbal communication can be ambiguous.

pouting: Sulking; a silent means of showing anger, resentment, or hurt.

power listening: The single most helpful thing you can do to help your partner deal with a problem. It consists of feedback to your partner showing your understanding of his or her message, usually including both the content of the message and your partner's feelings about the situation. This skill is also sometimes referred to as empathy, empathic listening, reflective listening, and active listening.

power listening lite: Any of four simple yet beneficial ways to encourage your partner to talk:

1. Door openers (e.g., "How'd it go today?" "Would you like to talk about it?" "What happened?")
2. "Attending," paying attention to, or being "with" your partner
3. Silence (not saying anything that interrupts your partner)
4. Empathic grunts ("Ummm" "Wow!" "No kidding?" "Really!" "Geez" "Uh-huh")

public criticism: Blameful or critical opinions of your partner that are expressed to a third person. A likely cause of hurt and humiliation in your partner and of damage to the relationship.

reflective listening: *See* power listening.

self-responsibility: Recognizing that you are the primary "need meeter" in your own life and that your partner's role in meeting your needs is both secondary and voluntary.

shared goal: A common goal shared by you and your partner. Also called "agreed-upon goal."

socialization: The process by which parents and other authority figures work to equip children with the skills needed to function successfully in society.

stonewalling: A condition caused by emotional and physiological over-load experienced by one partner during an argument in which he or she refuses or is unable to participate, answer questions, or respond. It results in that partner building up a defensive system that is impenetrable.

structure of a world class marriage: A diagram that shows the model for building a world class marriage. At the foundation are the three conditions that promote growth—empathy, acceptance, and genuineness. Upon this foundation are the 16 Pillars, which are specific behaviors that elevate relationships to world class status.

supportive climates: Behaviors or attitudes that set up an environment in which it is likely that your partner will feel safe and secure around you and comfortable being him- or herself in the relationship.

surrender: Making the decision to stop confronting your partner about a behavior or characteristic that he or she seems unable to change. Doing whatever work is necessary inside of yourself so that you can stop trying to change it without holding on to any resentment or hope for change.

three conditions that promote growth: These three conditions for growth—empathy, acceptance, and genuineness—were generated from the person-centered approach for psychotherapy in research by Carl Rogers.

"tit for tat": The use of "supposed fairness" as a means of manipulating your partner and making him or her "pay" for something that hurt you. Inflicting harm to retaliate—an eye for an eye, a blow for a blow—and justifying this on the basis of your partner inflicting the first hurt is all too common and results in increased damage to the relationship.

vulnerability: Being emotionally open and self-revealing. Being willing to communicate genuinely without blaming your partner or defending yourself. The essence of an XYZ confrontation is that it is emotionally open and arises from a willingness to be vulnerable to your partner.

XYZ message: The most effective way to confront your partner about a behavior that is unacceptable to you. It consists of three parts:

X: A nonblameful description of the behavior that is a problem for you.

Y: = The effects of that behavior on you.

Z: = Your feelings about those effects.

The strength of an I-Message is its self-revealing nature: it describes you, not your partner. This is also referred to as an I-Message.

BIBLIOGRAPHY

Arp, David, and Claudia Arp. *The Second Half of Marriage: Facing the Eight Challenges of Every Long-Term Marriage*. Grand Rapids, MI: Zondervan, 1996.

———. *52 Dates for You and Your Mate*. Nashville, TN: Thomas Nelson Publishers, 1993.

Berenson, Bernard G., and Robert R. Carkhuff. *Sources of Gain in Counseling and Psychotherapy*. New York: Holt, Rinehart and Winston, 1967.

Borysenko, Joan. *Minding the Body, Mending the Mind*. New York: Bantam Books, 1987.

Branden, Nathaniel. *Taking Responsibility: Self-Reliance and the Accountable Life*. New York: Simon & Schuster, 1996.

Canfield, Jack, Mark Victor Hansen, Mary and Chrissy Donnelly, and Barbara De Angelis. *Chicken Soup for the Couple's Soul: Inspirational Stories about Love and Relationships*. Deerfield Beach, FL: Health Communications, 1999.

Chapman, Gary. *The Five Love Languages: How to Express Heartfelt Commitment to Your Mate*. Chicago: Northfield Publishing, 1995.

Doherty, William J. *Take Back Your Marriage: Sticking Together in a World That Pulls Us Apart*. New York: The Guilford Press, 2001.

Evans, Patricia. *The Verbally Abusive Relationship: How to Recognize It and How to Respond*. New York: Adams Media, 1996.

Farrell, Warren. *Women Can't Hear What Men Don't Say: Destroying Myths, Creating Love.* New York: Jeremy P. Tarcher/Putnam, 1999.

Fisher, Roger, and William Ury. *Getting to Yes: Negotiating Agreement without Giving In.* New York: Penguin Books, 1983.

Gibb, J. R. "Defense Level and Influence Potential in Small Groups." In *Leadership and Interpersonal Behavior* edited by L. Petrullo and B. M. Bass. New York: Holt, Rinehart and Winston, 1961.

Godek, Gregory J. P. *1,001 Ways to Be Romantic.* Naperville, IL: Casablanca Press, 1995.

Gordon, Thomas. *L.E.T.: Leader Effectiveness Training: The No-Lose Way to Release the Productive Potential in People.* New York: Bantam, 1980.

———. *P.E.T.: Parent Effectiveness Training.* New York: New American Library, 1970.

Gottman, John. *Why Marriages Succeed or Fail . . . and How You Can Make Yours Last.* New York: Fireside, 1994.

Gottman, John, and Julie Schwartz Gottman. *And Baby Makes Three.* New York: Crown Publishers, 2007.

Gottman, John, Cliff Notarious, Jonni Gonso, and Howard Markman. *A Couple's Guide to Communication.* Champaign, IL: Research Press, 1976.

Gottman, John, and Nan Silver. *The Seven Principles for Making Marriage Work.* New York: Crown Publishers, 1999.

Harley, Willard F. *Buyers, Renters & Freeloaders: Turning Revolving-Door Romance into Lasting Love.* Grand Rapids, MI: Fleming H. Revell, 2002.

Hendrix, Harville. *Getting the Love You Want: A Guide for Couples.* New York: Harper & Row, 1990.

Hendrix, Harville, and Helen Hunt. *The Couples Companion: Meditations and Exercises for Getting the Love You Want.* New York: Pocket Books, 1994.

Hopson, Derek S., and Darlene Powell Hopson. *Friends, Lovers and Soulmates: A Guide to Better Relationships between Black Men and Women.* New York: Fireside, 1994.

Johnson, Sue. *Hold Me Tight: Seven Conversations for a Lifetime of Love.* New York: Little, Brown and Company, 2008.

Jourard, Sidney M. *The Transparent Self.* Princeton, NJ: D. Van Nostrand Company, 1964.

Love, Patricia, and Jo Robinson. *Hot Monogamy: Essential Steps to More Passionate, Intimate Lovemaking.* New York: Plume, 1994.

McCarthy, Barry, and Emily McCarthy. *Couple Sexual Awareness: Building Sexual Happiness.* New York: Carroll & Graf Publishers, 1998.

———. *Sexual Awareness: Couple Sexuality for the Twenty-First Century.* New York: Carroll & Graf Publishers, 1993.

Perel, Esther. *Mating in Captivity: Unlocking Erotic Intelligence.* New York: Harper, 2006.

Rogers, Carl R. *Client-Centered Therapy.* Boston, MA: Houghton Mifflin Company, 1951.

———. *On Becoming a Person: A Therapist's View of Psychotherapy.* New York: Houghton Mifflin Company, 1961.

———. *A Way of Being.* New York: Houghton Mifflin Company, 1980.

Schnarch, David. *Passionate Marriage: Love, Sex and Intimacy in Emotionally Committed Relationships.* New York: Owl Books, 1998.

Sotile, Wayne M., and Mary O. Sotile. *Marriage Skills for Busy Couples: How to Avoid Supercouple Syndrome.* Winston-Salem, NC: Real Talk, 1998.

Waite, Linda J., and Maggie Gallagher. *The Case for Marriage: Why Married People Are Happier, Healthier, and Better off Financially.* New York: Doubleday, 2000.

Wallerstein, Judith S., and Sandra Blakeslee. *The Good Marriage: How & Why Love Lasts.* New York: Warner Books, 1995.

Weiner-Davis, Michele. *Divorce Busting: A Step-by-Step Approach to Making Your Marriage Loving Again.* New York: Fireside, 1992.

Wemhoff, Rich, ed. *Marriage: The Best Resources to Help Yours Thrive.* Seattle: Resource Pathways, 1999.

WORKSHOPS

Want to increase your ability to apply the 16 Pillars of a world class marriage? Or would you like to be trained to offer World Class Marriage workshops in your community?

In California, World Class Marriage workshops for couples and train-the-facilitator workshops are offered through the California Healthy Marriages Coalition. For more information and registration, visit www.camarriage.com.

Outside of California, for information about World Class Marriage workshops for couples and train-the-facilitator workshops, e-mail HJTrainings@aol.com or call (760) 436-3960. Visit our Web site at www.worldclassmarriage.com.

INDEX

ABOUT THE AUTHORS

Patty Howell and Ralph Jones have taught relationship skills in fourteen countries throughout the world. Together they founded Howell-Jones Trainings in 1995 to develop and deliver programs and products that enrich relationships and support people's health, happiness, and productivity.

Patty Howell, Ed.M., A.G.C., is a nationally recognized marriage and relationship educator who serves as vice president of operations and media relations for the California Healthy Marriages Coalition, a pioneering nonprofit that works throughout California to increase awareness about marriage and relationship education. A popular public speaker, Patty is the author of many programs and publications including the highly esteemed "Healthy Marriages" series of booklets for which she was honored in 2010 with the Smart Marriages Impact Award. She was the founding president of Pacific Rim Park, a nonprofit organization that fosters international cooperation and good will.

Ralph Jones has been a prominent trainer in the person-centered approach for more than thirty years. Working with Dr. Thomas Gordon, he oversaw the expansion of Gordon Training programs into a worldwide phenomenon. Ralph has taught hundreds of communication workshops for professionals and laypeople around the world and is responsible for the creation of training materials now used on four continents. He currently works in training and human resources with the California Healthy Marriages Coalition.

Ralph and Patty, husband and wife as well as training and writing partners, live in San Diego and have enjoyed the benefits of a world class marriage for more than thirty years.

INTERNATIONAL EDITIONS

China
World Class Marriage [in Chinese] (Chongqing: Chongqing Publishing House, 2003).

－与伴侣亲密
相处的法则

France
Couple: vivre et grandir ensemble (Paris: Marabout-Hachette, 2002).

Germany
Der Kleine Beziehungs-therapeut (Stuttgart: Klett-Cotta, 2003; Munich: Deutscher Taschenbuch Verlag, 2007).

Hungary
Ötcsillagos házasság (Budapest: Magyar Könyvklub, 2002).

Italy
Relazione di Coppia Efficace (Bari: Edizioni La Meridiana, 2005).

Korea

World Class Marriage [in Korean] (Seoul: HOME International, 2008), (Leucadia, CA: HJBooks, 2009).

ㅣ등급 결혼

Mexico

Matrimonio de Clase Mundial (Mexico City: Editorial Diana, 2002), (Leucadia, CA: HJBooks, 2009).

Netherlands

Partners! Samen werken aan een inspirerende relatie (Baarn: Tirion Uitgevers BV, 2001).

Poland

Malzenstwo Na Medal (Warsaw: Jak Stworzyc Wymarzony Zwiazek, 2004).

Russia

World Class Marriage (Vladivostok: Far-Eastern State Technical University, 2002).